JENNIFER ARMS

SHIPWRECK AT THE BOTTOM OF THE WORLD

THE EXTRAORDINARY TRUE STORY OF SHACKLETON AND THE ENDURANCE

SCHOLASTIC INC.

New York Toronto London Auckland Sydney
Mexico City New Delhi Hong Kong

For Jim: I'd go to the ends of the earth for you.

Photographs courtesy of the Scott Polar Research Institute

Maps by Kayley LeFaiver

ISBN 0-439-10992-2

12 11 10 9 8 7 6 5 4 3 2 1   9/9 0 1 2 3 4/0

Printed in the U.S.A.   23

First Scholastic printing, November 1999

CONTENTS

Holness   Bakewell

Stevenson   How

McNeish   James   Wild   Worsley   Hudson   Green

Cheetham   Crean   Hussey   Greenstreet   Shackleton   Gooch   Rickinson   Hurley

Clark   Wordie   Macklin   Marston   McIlroy

Members of the expedition during the voyage south. Missing from this photograph are Blackborrow, Kerr, McCarthy, McLeod, Orde-Lees, and Vincent. Daniel Gooch, seated next to Shackleton, left the ship in South Georgia.

MEMBERS OF THE IMPERIAL TRANS-ANTARCTIC EXPEDITION

Sir Ernest Shackleton	Leader
Frank Wild	Second-in-Command
Frank Worsley	Captain of *Endurance*
Hubert Hudson	Navigating Officer
Lionel Greenstreet	First Officer
Thomas Crean	Second Officer
Alfred Cheetham	Third Officer
Louis Rickinson	Chief Engineer
A.J. Kerr	Second Engineer
Dr. James McIlroy	Surgeon
Dr. Alexander Macklin	Surgeon
Robert Clark	Biologist
Leonard Hussey	Meteorologist
James Wordie	Geologist
Reginald James	Physicist
George Marston	Artist
Thomas Orde-Lees	Motor Expert
Frank Hurley	Expedition Photographer
Harry McNeish	Carpenter
Charles Green	Cook
Percy Blackborrow	Steward
John Vincent	Able Seaman
Timothy McCarthy	Able Seaman
Walter How	Able Seaman
William Bakewell	Able Seaman
Thomas McLeod	Able Seaman
William Stevenson	Fireman
Ernest Holness	Fireman

ENDURANCE

The original plans of *Endurance*. Built in Norway, the ship was 144 feet long and 25 feet wide. There were four decks: the bridge deck, from which the ship was steered; the main deck, containing the saloon and the officers' cabins; the lower deck, containing the engine room and crew's quarters; and the hold, where coal, fresh water, and provisions were stored.

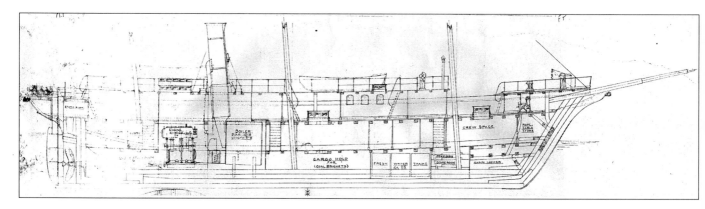

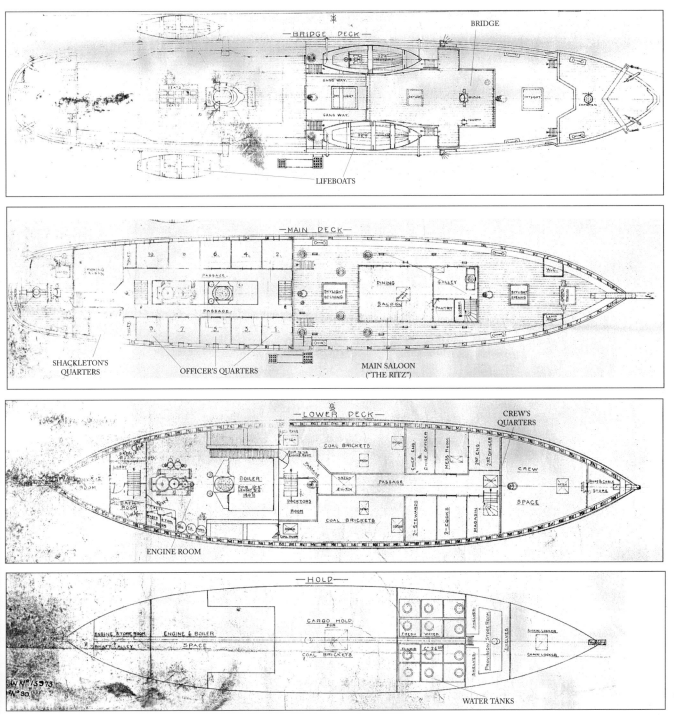

BRIDGE

BRIDGE DECK

GANG WAY.

GANG WAY.

LIFEBOATS

MAIN DECK

10 8 6 4 2

PASSAGE

PASSAGE.

9 7 5 3 1

DINING
SALOON

GALLEY

PANTRY

W.C.

SKYLIGHT
OPENING

SKYLIGHT
OPENING

SHACKLETON'S
QUARTERS

OFFICER'S QUARTERS

MAIN SALOON
("THE RITZ")

LOWER DECK

CREW'S
QUARTERS

COAL BRICKETS

BOILER

DOCTOR'S
ROOM

COAL BRICKETS

PASSAGE

CHIEF ENG.

CHIEF OFFICER

MESS ROOM

2ND ENG.

2ND OFFICER

CREW

SPACE

2 STEWARDS

2 COOKS

MAGAZIN

ROPE & CABLE
STORE

ENGINE ROOM

HOLD

ENGINE STORE ROOM

SHAFT ALLEY

ENGINE & BOILER

SPACE

CARGO HOLD
FOR

COAL BRICKETS

FRESH WATER

PROVISION STORE ROOM

CHAIN LOCKER

CHAIN LOCKER

WATER TANKS

COURTESY OF THE NATIONAL MARITIME MUSEUM, GREENWICH

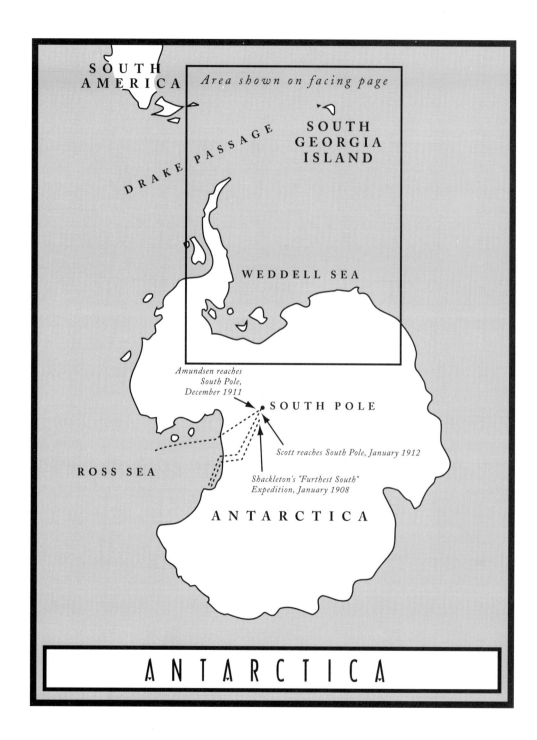

SOUTH
AMERICA

Area shown on facing page

DRAKE PASSAGE

SOUTH
GEORGIA
ISLAND

WEDDELL SEA

Amundsen reaches
South Pole,
December 1911

SOUTH POLE

Scott reaches South Pole, January 1912

ROSS SEA

Shackleton's "Furthest South"
Expedition, January 1908

ANTARCTICA

ANTARCTICA

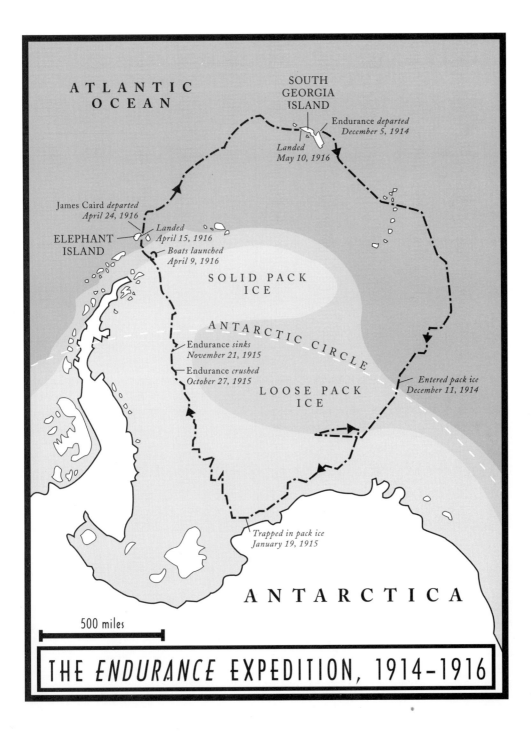

ATLANTIC
OCEAN

SOUTH
GEORGIA
ISLAND

*Endurance departed
December 5, 1914*

*Landed
May 10, 1916*

James Caird *departed
April 24, 1916*

*Landed
April 15, 1916*

ELEPHANT
ISLAND

*Boats launched
April 9, 1916*

SOLID PACK
ICE

ANTARCTIC CIRCLE

*Endurance sinks
November 21, 1915*

*Endurance crushed
October 27, 1915*

LOOSE PACK
ICE

*Entered pack ice
December 11, 1914*

*Trapped in pack ice
January 19, 1915*

ANTARCTICA

500 miles

THE *ENDURANCE* EXPEDITION, 1914–1916

"For scientific discovery, give me Scott; for speed and efficiency of travel, give me Amundsen; but when disaster strikes and all hope is gone, get down on your knees and pray for Shackleton."

Apsley Cherry-Garrard, polar explorer, 1922

JUST IMAGINE

Just imagine yourself in the most hostile place on earth. It's not the Sahara or the Gobi Desert. It's not the Arctic. The most hostile place on earth is the Antarctic, the location of the South Pole. North Pole, South Pole—what's the difference? The Arctic is mostly water—with ice on top, of course—and that ice is never more than a few feet thick. But under the South Pole lies a continent that supports glaciers up to two miles in depth. Almost the entire southern continent is covered by ice. This mammoth icecap presses down so heavily that it actually distorts the shape of the earth. The ice never melts; it clings to the bottom of the world, spawning winds, storms, and weather that affect the whole planet.

And of all the weather it creates, the weather the Antarctic creates for itself is by far the worst. In the winter, the temperature can sink to 100 degrees below zero Fahrenheit. Cold air masses sliding down the sides of the glaciers speed up until they become winds of close to 200 miles per hour. When winter descends on the southern continent, the seas surrounding the land begin to freeze at the terrifying rate of two square miles every minute, until the frozen sea reaches an area of 7 million square miles, about twice the size of the United States. It is truly the most hostile environment this side of the moon. Just imagine yourself stranded in such a place.

In 1915, a British crew of twenty-eight men *was* stranded there, with no ship and no way to contact the outside world. They all survived.

THE IMPERIAL TRANS-ANTARCTIC EXPEDITION

Ernest Henry Shackleton knew all about the weather in the Antarctic. In 1908, Shackleton had been the first explorer to come within 100 miles of the South Pole. On his triumphal return from that journey, he was rewarded with a knighthood for his efforts. He was a world-famous celebrity, a hero to thousands who read his thrilling book on his "Furthest South" expedition. He was determined to try again for the conquest of the South Pole, but before he could organize a new expedition, two other explorers headed for the frozen continent. In 1911, the Norwegian explorer Roald Amundsen reached the Pole. Only five weeks later, Captain Robert F. Scott of England reached it, a heartbreaking second-place finish—and then died on the way back to his base. All of England mourned the death of Captain Scott. Now that the South Pole had been reached, it seemed as though the age of heroic exploration was over. And yet was it?

Antarctica had never even been sighted before the nineteenth century. Until then it was a rumor, an undefined, unseen question mark shrouded in fog and surrounded by ice. But it hadn't always hidden at the bottom of the world behind a veil of frozen mist. One hundred sixty million years ago, Antarctica was part of the supercontinent Gondwana, which also included South America, Africa, and Australia. The Jurassic climate of Gondwana was semitropical, and fossils from Antarctica prove that the continent was once inhabited by giant flightless birds, sharks and freshwater fish, snails, beetles, reptiles, and protomarsupials, all thriving under giant ferns and trees.

The supercontinent began to break apart, however, and by 60 million years ago, Antarctica had migrated south to its present location over the Pole. In a mere 20 million years, the continent was covered with ice, and the environment had become too hostile for most living things.

By modern times, only one percent of the continent was free of ice. But not only was it too cold for most life, it was also too dry, with an annual rain and snowfall of only two inches per year—the same as that of the Australian outback. The polar icecap had made Antarctica a frozen desert.

"The Boss." Sir Ernest Henry Shackleton, leader of the Imperial Trans-Antarctic Expedition, had already been to the Antarctic twice before setting out on *Endurance*.

The cold air masses created by this icecap clash with the warm winds from the ocean to churn up a storm belt that surrounds the continent, making the Southern Ocean the most treacherous sea anywhere. The southern latitudes—from forty degrees south latitude to the Antarctic Circle at sixty-seven degrees south latitude—long ago earned their nicknames from the sailors who dared approach the continent: the Roaring Forties, the Furious Fifties, and the Screaming Sixties. Countless ships have been lost in these waters. Countless sailors have lost their lives.

These perilous seas kept the continent locked away until 1774, when Captain James Cook reached the farthest south latitude yet attained. He wormed his ship through the ice pack to reach seventy-one degrees south latitude, and then turned north again without ever seeing the land. In 1820, a Russian Navy ship under the command of Fabian Gottlieb von Bellingshausen made the first circumnavigation and sighting of the continent. Twenty years later, James Ross became the first to bull all the way through the pack to reach land. As the nineteenth century ran out, more and more of the continent was mapped and described by navigators from around the world—although Antarctica claimed many ships as payment. By the turn of the century the fringes of the continent were fairly well defined on the charts, but the interior was still an unknown wasteland of ice.

Then came the race to the South Pole. Shackleton's attempt in 1908 ended when he was thrown back by terrible weather conditions only ninety-seven miles from his goal. The prize ultimately went to Amundsen on December 14, 1911, and Scott stumbled to the Pole just over than a month later, on January 17, 1912. And there were still 5.5 million square miles untouched by man—an area twenty-five percent larger than the continent of Europe.

All of England—including Shackleton—regretted losing the honor of being first at the Pole. But Shackleton set his sights on a new goal: to be the first to cross the southern continent from one side to the other. There was indeed much more exploring to be done.

On December 29, 1913, the London *Times* trumpeted: "We are able to announce today, with a satisfaction which shall be universally shared, that Sir Ernest Shackleton will lead a new expedition to the South Pole next year."

Lord Curzon, president of the Royal Geographical Society, summed up the feelings of most of Shackleton's fans: "That it is a task worthy to be undertaken by an Englishman is to me quite clear; and that of living Englishmen you are the best fitted by training, experience, and prestige to carry it out successfully none will be found to deny."

Even without such support, however, Shackleton had to go to Antarctica again, because the continent pulled him like a magnet. "I am just good as an explorer and nothing else," he wrote to his wife, Emily. He had been bitten hard by the exploration bug.

An Irishman by birth, the forty-year-old Shackleton was a showman with a hunger for polar glory. As a child, he had been something of a loner, reading adventure stories during his school days and dreaming of fame and fortune. At sixteen he joined the merchant marine, and his first voyage took him around Cape Horn in the winter: it was his first experience of the Southern Ocean. By 1900, at age twenty-six, he had risen in the ranks of the merchant service, carrying mail and cargo around the British Empire. But he worried that his routine voyages might, in fact, be a dead end. Citing his years of experience at sea, he presented himself at the offices of the National Antarctic Expedition in London. In 1901, as a junior officer aboard the *Discovery*, captained by Robert F. Scott, he headed for Antarctica for the first time.

There was no going back, for Shackleton. He had found his true calling. After *Discovery* came his "Furthest South" expedition in 1908. Now, in 1914, he was famous enough as an Antarctic explorer to be able to raise the money he needed for his new journey. He even had the commercial smarts to form a film syndicate, based on the fame of his expedition photographer, an Australian named Frank Hurley. Shackleton sweet-talked wealthy patrons, took public donations, and raised money as an advance based on future sales of film and photo rights. He also retained the rights to all crew diaries, with the aim of publishing them at the end of a successful trip.

With this bankroll, he was able to purchase and outfit a three-masted, coal-powered barkentine called *Polaris* from a Norwegian firm that specialized in polar vessels. Its thick wooden hull was specially designed for plowing through polar ice packs: in some places it was more than four feet thick, but the wood

Members of Shackleton's crew: *Top,* Frank Wild, second-in-command, and second officer Tom Crean (with some of the sled-dog puppies born during the expedition). *Bottom,* Frank Hurley, expedition photographer, and Frank Worsley, captain of *Endurance.*

was still flexible enough to withstand the squeezing of polar ice. The ship was capable of doing nine to ten knots under steam. In honor of his family motto, "By endurance we conquer," Shackleton rechristened the ship *Endurance.*

There was no need to call for volunteers to join the Imperial Trans-Antarctic Expedition. Almost as soon as the expedition was announced, 5,000 would-be explorers rushed to the expedition's office on New Burlington Street in London to join. Letters poured in from people all over the world, including at least one woman and a fifteen-year-old boy. Some letters were simply addressed SIR ERNEST SHACKLETON, LONDON.

From this flood of volunteers, Shackleton began to pick a crew. Some of the leader's choices for his team were obvious. Frank Wild, his second-in-command, had been with him on his two previous journeys south and had spent a total of six years in Antarctica, logging more than 5,000 miles of sledging. Tom Crean, another Irishman and a tough sailor, had also been south with Shackleton before, and proudly wore Britain's snow-white Polar Medal on his jacket. (Crean had also served with Captain Scott; it was Crean who found Scott's lifeless body after the explorer's second-place finish at the Pole.) George Marston, the official artist of the expedition, had adventured in the Antarctic with Shackleton, too. Frank Hurley, the twenty-four-year-old photographer, had been to the Antarctic with an explorer named Douglas Mawson, and was a key member because of the financial backing he could attract. Alfred Cheetham had served under Scott in the Antarctic, along with Crean. A merchant marine officer named Frank Worsley, a part-Maori New Zealander who had been a sailor since the age of sixteen, was to captain the ship.

The rest of the crew was made up of able seamen accustomed to the harsh weather of the North Sea, two doctors, a handful of university scientists, officers, a carpenter, and a cook. For seamen the yearly salary was fifty pounds; for scientists it was 150. Some of the men had polar experience, either Arctic or Antarctic. Some of the men had never been out of England before, let alone imagined a voyage to the southern continent. But whatever their experience, whether North Sea trawler-hand or Cambridge University scientist, they knew they were in for the adventure of a lifetime.

Endurance now had a crew. In the ship's hold were stores for at least two years, including a recent innovation: concentrated Bovril sledging rations for the trans-Antarctic run on dogsleds. Worsley explained that this mixture "was composed of lard, oatmeal, beef protein, vegetable protein, salt, and sugar. The result was heating, nourishing, and antiscorbutic [scurvy-preventing], and it was invaluable. Made up in half-pound bricks for one man's meal, it had the consistency of a new cheese and a yellow-brown color, but looked, when boiled with water, like thick pea soup." Scurvy, the depletion of vitamin C, or ascorbic acid, had always been a problem on long voyages and had contributed to Captain Scott's death en route from the South Pole. Shackleton had consulted the British Army's nutritionist, who believed in the newfangled idea of vitamins and who helped concoct the rations. Each brick consisted of 2,864 calories and was wrapped in wax paper and packed in tin boxes; the hold of the ship was loaded with them.

In addition to these sledging rations were powdered milk and cocoa, sugar, tea, potatoes, tobacco, canned meats and vegetables, liquor, flour, and a dozen and one other staples and delicacies. Shackleton believed in keeping his men well fed.

The ship also carried coal, rifles, ammunition, scientific apparatus, a radio, games, books, navigational charts, lanterns, tanks and cages for bringing back live seals and penguins, three lifeboats and a small landing boat, a miniature billiard table, typewriters, sleeping bags, tents, matches, lumber for a hut, a bicycle, a motor-propelled sledge and dogsleds, two gramophones, skis, a sewing machine, hockey skates, soccer balls, the meteorologist's banjo, and the carpenter's cat, Mrs. Chippy.

The plan for the Imperial Trans-Antarctic Expedition was this: *Endurance* would sail from South America into the Weddell Sea, which is bordered by the Antarctic Peninsula. This peninsula, part of the same geological formation as the Andes Mountains, reaches north from Antarctica like an outstretched arm, cradling the Weddell Sea. Having crossed the Weddell Sea, Shackleton would make landfall at the best opportunity, and then set out across the continent. At the same time that *Endurance* left South America, a sister ship called *Aurora* would sail from Australia and wait on the opposite side of Antarctica to pick up Shackleton and his hand-picked overland team at the end of a triumphant five-month trek. The *Aurora* team would also trek inland, laying down stores of food for Shackleton's group to pick up and use on their final run to the coast.

The expedition's main object, explained in the fund-raising brochure, was "to cross the Antarctic from sea to sea, securing for the British flag the honor of being the first carried across the South Polar Continent." That, in a patriotic nutshell, was the plan. That was what was *supposed* to happen. Many of the details of how the expedition would be carried out were unspecified. Like many explorers of his day, Shackleton was a great believer in improvisation: he would figure things out as the need arose. As long as he was well equipped and had a good crew, he was confident in his ability to pull off his plan.

At her dock on the River Thames in London, *Endurance* became a major tourist attraction. Curious sightseers came from far and wide to view the celebrity ship and its daring crew. The attention was welcomed by the men, who answered hundreds of questions. Alfred Cheetham, the third officer, found himself in conversation with some women who wondered about the dangers ahead, and about Shackleton's ability to lead the men through unforeseen perils. "Aye, he's a fine leader, he is," Cheetham replied. "He don't run you into any danger if he can help it; but, by gum! if there's danger, he goes first."

In July, Queen Alexandra made a royal tour of inspection of *Endurance* at the dock in London and presented Shackleton and his crew with an inscribed Bible. To Shackleton she also gave a Union Jack (a British flag) and a silver and enamel medallion of St. Christopher, the patron saint of ferrymen. The queen's sister, Empress Marie of Russia, took photographs during the royal inspection, and afterward, the eager fans who mobbed the dock gave the crew teddy bears and other mascots to carry south. The great Amundsen himself sent a telegram that read: MY WARMEST WISHES FOR YOUR MAGNIFICENT UNDERTAKING. By August 1, 1914, *Endurance* and her crew were ready to leave for the Southern Hemisphere.

THE GROWLERS

As *Endurance* steamed down the River Thames toward the sea, however, World War I boiled up in Europe. Great Britain was preparing to join the war against Germany. Shackleton had no choice but to telegraph the Admiralty and place the entire ship, crew, and stores at the Royal Navy's disposal. Two military members of the crew immediately resigned from the expedition to rejoin their regiments. Shackleton and the rest of the men on board *Endurance* were tortured by indecision: they were all patriotic subjects of a country heading into war, and yet they all now burned to voyage south. They waited anxiously for word of their fate. At last, Winston Churchill, who was First Lord of the Admiralty at the time, sent a telegram: PROCEED.

On August 8, the Imperial Trans-Antarctic Expedition left England behind. With mixed emotions the crew watched England's shores slip away. On the eve of Britain's entry into war, every man knew he was leaving his country at a critical time, and would be out of all contact for at least a year and a half. But they set sail, nevertheless. There would be no turning back. As Shackleton wrote home in a telegram: WE ARE LEAVING NOW TO CARRY ON OUR WHITE WARFARE.

By October they were in Buenos Aires, on the coast of Argentina, where there was some shuffling of the crew: a few of the original members were discharged for drunkenness, and replacements were hired on the spot. Argentine sightseers crowded the docks to see the world-famous explorers, and showered the crew with invitations to dinners, dances, and cabarets. A motley pack of sixty-nine half-wild sled dogs from Canada was brought on board. Not a single member of the crew had any experience of driving a dog team, but that wasn't the sort of detail to worry the confident Shackleton. The dogs were housed in kennels built on deck, where they snapped and lunged at anyone who passed too close. The Argentine Naval Band played the British and Argentine national anthems with an accompaniment of barking, growling, snarling, and howling from the dogs as *Endurance* set sail on the next leg of the voyage. It was October 26, 1914.

Unbeknownst to the commander, the ship carried an additional newcomer. A young sailor named Percy Blackborrow was hiding in a locker, aided by William Bakewell, another young seaman. Once the ship was three days out from Buenos Aires and there was no chance of returning, Blackborrow was brought forward to face a furious commander. As Mrs. Chippy, the cat, rubbed against Shackleton's legs, the commander looked the stowaway up and down.

"Do you know that on these expeditions we often get very hungry, and if there is a stowaway available he is the first to be eaten?" he warned, ignoring the cat purring at his feet.

Percy Blackborrow, the stowaway, with Mrs. Chippy (who was actually a tomcat). After Blackborrow was brought before the Boss, he was made the ship's steward.

Blackborrow was not dismayed. "They'd get a lot more meat off you, sir!"

Shackleton turned away to hide a grin and told Frank Wild to turn the lad over to the bo'sun, but added, "Introduce him to the cook first!"

The crew was somewhat in awe of their commander, whom they all called Boss. As Dr. James McIlroy said, "Shackleton could be a very frightening kind of individual; like Napoleon, he was very stern-looking and fixed you with a steely eye." In the months that followed, they would learn to follow him almost without question. Shackleton was a master at keeping his crew working together. Whenever he found two men who had quarreled and were not speaking to each other, he told them, "Stop and forget it," and made them shake hands. He never let them forget that their strength lay in unity.

Because seasons are reversed in the Southern Hemisphere, spring was well under way as the coast of South America slipped away to the northwest. *Endurance* headed for South Georgia Island, one of the Subantarctic Islands on the edge of the Antarctic Convergence. The convergence, also called the polar front, is where frigid, oxygen-rich water from the south (cold water holds more oxygen than warm water) mixes with warmer water from the north, causing a thermal swap or slow churning in the water that pulls nutrients up from the ocean floor. This shifting front of rich ocean, about twenty-five miles wide, is the most fertile ecosystem in the world, supporting awesome numbers of fish, seabirds, seals, and whales.

Whaling first brought people to South Georgia Island, and it was to a whaling station that *Endurance* headed as its final stop before challenging the Antarctic. Grytviken was a Norwegian outpost on Stromness Bay, a natural harbor at the base of the island's rugged alpine cliffs and glaciers. Snow squalls and heavy seas made visibility poor and forced *Endurance* to creep forward with the engines dead slow as it headed into Stromness Bay. A whaling boat was spotted in the fog, and *Endurance* gave two blasts of its whistle. Immediately, the *Sitka* came alongside *Endurance* and, with a whale carcass acting as a bumper between the two vessels in the heavy waves, piloted the ship into Grytviken. *Endurance* landed at South Georgia Island on November 5, three months after leaving England.

The whaling station was a rough spot, with the carcasses of blue and

Grytviken whaling station on South Georgia Island. The whaling station employed approximately 200 men of different nationalities, although most of them were Norwegian. Tons of whale meat, bone, and scrap blubber lay rotting around the station.

humpback whales putrefying in the midnight sun, and the harbor red with blood and shimmering with grease around the oil factory. Billowing clouds of steam rose from the plant where blubber was being boiled down. According to Harry McNeish, the ship's Scottish carpenter, "Ye could snuff the aroma if ye were five miles out to wind'ard." The crew soon gave the harbor the sarcastic name "the Scent Bottle." From the mountainsides echoed the harsh donkey bray of gentoo penguins, the screech of skuas, and the bellowing of elephant seals. When *Endurance* docked at Grytviken, the Canadian wolf dogs were let off to gorge themselves on whale meat, and they added their barking and snarling to the din that echoed from the Alps of the Southern Ocean.

The Norwegian whalers were the only source of information about current conditions in the Antarctic, and the news they had for Shackleton was bad. The ice pack surrounding the continent had been particularly heavy that year, and it wasn't breaking up as quickly as usual. None of the experienced whalers could remember ever seeing the pack so far north. "A bad year for ice" was the terse description Shackleton heard over and over. Although he had planned to stay at Grytviken only a short while, the Boss decided to wait one or two weeks longer for the warm weather to break up the ice.

Meanwhile, the crew made the most of their time ashore. Hurley was fearless in scaling the cliffs around the harbor in the pursuit of great photographs (and he had to lug around a large box camera to do it). Some of the men prac-

A blue whale being "flensed" at Grytviken. The whalers strip the carcass of blubber and boil it down into oil. According to Hussey, the harbor had a "most appalling stench" from the dead whales moored in the harbor awaiting flensing.

Bull elephant seals on South Georgia Island. Meteorologist Leonard Hussey described the noise that sleeping elephant seals make as "suggestive of a nightmare or a guilty conscience. The inspirations of the breath are irregular gasps, the expirations tremulous wheezes. The body shakes violently from time to time, and the foreflippers are ever nervously moving about."

ticed skiing. Because they were so far south, the sun shone around the clock, and the crew was resourceful in finding entertainment. There were practical jokes, including one on Hubert Hudson, the navigator, who was generally considered an oddball and a sitting duck for jokes. Told there was a costume party ashore, Hudson was persuaded to dress in a bedsheet with a teapot lid tied with ribbons to his head. In this bizarre getup, Hudson made a grand entrance into a party at the whaling station, only to find himself the sole person in costume. From then on, Hudson was nicknamed Buddha.

In all, *Endurance* spent a month at Grytviken. Each day of delay meant putting the expedition in jeopardy, however. If Shackleton did not reach the edge of the continent before the end of the short Antarctic summer, the ice would shut him out. On the advice of the whalers, Shackleton had the decks of *Endurance* loaded with extra coal for ramming through the ice. Then, on December 5, a little more than two weeks before Midsummer's Day, *Endurance* set sail from Grytviken. Huge, dripping slabs of bloody whale meat meant for dog food hung from the rigging out of reach of the animals. Behind them, the whaling factory blasted its whistle and saluted the ship with rounds of harpoon-gun fire. *Endurance* was on its way to the frozen continent.

Only three days later they met their first ice, large chunks called growlers that scraped and rumbled past the sides of the ship. The Norwegians had been

A view of the interior of South Georgia Island, the "Alps of the Southern Ocean." When the crew landed here, no one had ever tried climbing across these forbidding mountains and glaciers. The figure in the foreground is Worsley.

right. The ice had never before been seen so far north. They were still 600 miles from the nearest coastline and hadn't even crossed the Antarctic Circle. Yet ahead to the south in the Weddell Sea, brilliant blue icebergs shone in the polar sun like the walls and ramparts of a fortress.

THE FIST OF THE ANTARCTIC

For the rest of December, *Endurance* picked her way through the ice. Blackborrow peeled a page from the calendar in the wardroom every morning, counting off the days. Outside, the ocean teemed with life. Humpbacks and killer whales spouted in the distance, and the water was dotted with ice floes on which fat, blinking seals basked in the sun. Emperor penguins bowed formally to the ship and crew as they passed. Adélie penguins surveyed them from passing icebergs and called, "Clark! Clark!"—which was the name of the expedition's biologist. The little black Adélies, with a shocking white ring around their eyes, made a comical sight for the crew as they tobogganed off the icebergs into the water. Flocks of Antarctic petrels and snow petrels accompanied the ship on its journey toward the continent, diving with high, wild screams when the crew threw their garbage overboard into the sea. While white albatrosses escorted *Endurance* through the ice on their magnificent, motionless wings, Leonard Hussey, the meteorologist, serenaded the passing wildlife with his banjo.

McNeish remarked that the penguins were particularly attracted to the banjo music. "Ay, they're queer creatures, an' ah'd never have been surprised tae see them clappin' their flippers when the doctor finished a tune. When he played guid old Scots tunes, that was. They're sensible birds; they liked real music. But, ah can tell ye that if he played anything else they'd break away an' rush off in a panic."

Hussey's version of the penguins' taste was somewhat different. "They liked Negro spirituals and Irish jigs. A strong favorite of which they never tired was 'It's a Long, Long Way to Tipperary.' But when I turned to playing Scottish music—well, they just fled in horror, making off as fast as their short legs would carry them."

The animals on board provided entertainment, too. Mrs. Chippy (who, despite his name, was actually a tomcat) discovered that he could stroll along the tops of the dog kennels just out of reach of the snapping jaws. The half-wolf sled dogs became frantic with bloodlust whenever the cat ambled by over head. Also on board were two pigs purchased by McNeish for future pork roasts, as well as the rats and mice that stow away on any ship. Mrs. Chippy was too well fed to bother hunting, preferring to torment the dogs and dine on scraps from the galley.

The ship made progress, but slow progress. Shackleton had estimated a rate of travel that would put him on the continent by the end of December, but by Christmas they still hadn't passed the Antarctic Circle. The holiday was celebrated with turtle soup, jugged hare, whitebait (a type of fish), mince pies, figs, and plum pudding prepared by the cook, Charles Green. When the crew raised their glasses of stout and rum to Christmas carols and toasted "To our sweethearts and wives," the answer came back, "May they never meet!"

As the last days of 1914 ran out, *Endurance* continued to creep southward through the Weddell Sea. The course was never a straight one. Sometimes the ship found a lead of open water to the south and followed that with all speed. Other times, Worsley, the skipper, had to sail the ship west along the edge of the pack searching for open water to enter, even sailing north from time to time when the pack was impenetrable, or standing still, waiting for a lead. Feeling like a rat in a trap, Worsley looked for leads from the crow's-nest and signaled the course to the man on the bridge. Iceblink, a white glare on the underside of the clouds, indicated pack ice ahead. A water sky, a dark reflection on the clouds, showed where the open water lay.

Shackleton explained, "Worsley, Wild, and I, with three officers, kept three watches while we were working through the pack, so that we had two officers on deck all the time. The carpenter had rigged a six-foot wooden semaphore on the bridge to enable the navigating officer to give the seamen or scientists at the wheel the direction and the exact amount of helm required. This device saved time as well as the effort of shouting."

Occasionally, when the frigid atmosphere was charged with water, every rope and spar on the ship was frosted white, making *Endurance* look like another species of sparkling white iceberg as it nosed its way through the pack. When the sun came out, icicles fell from the shrouds and shattered like glass on the decks below. Sometimes open leads of water in all directions were wreathed with wisps of frost smoke as the water began to freeze, and

Endurance begins to pick its way through the ice, December 9, 1914. Shackleton wrote in his diary: "I had been prepared for evil conditions in the Weddell Sea, but had hoped that in December and January the pack would be loose, even if no open water was to be found. What we were encountering was fairly dense pack of a very obstinate nature."

"To our sweethearts and wives—may they never meet!"

Shackleton commented that the effect resembled the smoke from a prairie fire. The sun never set, and even when there was fog it was never dark. Often the crystalline air formed mirages, and the sailors saw icebergs suspended upside down on the horizon. These mirages made navigation around the bergs very dangerous, because it was often hard to tell what was a real iceberg and what was a phantom. Knowing the difference was critical, especially since *Endurance* often passed more than 400 bergs in a twenty-four-hour period: it was a crowded sea.

On New Year's Eve, they crossed the Antarctic Circle at last, and some of the men gathered on the bridge to sing "Auld Lang Syne" with an accompaniment of dog howls. The ice grew denser, and open water became harder and harder to find. There was no sign that the pack was opening up at all. Day and night, ice growled and scraped along the sides of the ship. The men heard it grinding while they slept, while they ate or played cards, while they stoked the engines or read the charts.

When fog and ice made progress impossible, Shackleton ordered the ship moored to a large iceberg or floe. Then the men and dogs could take advantage of the wide, flat floes to get some exercise. Hockey and soccer games were the sport of choice among the men. As for the dogs, they could chase penguins and run wild without going too far—on all sides was the frigid sea, where killer whales cruised in search of a meal. "These beasts have a habit of locating a resting seal by looking over the edge of a floe, and then striking through the ice from below in search of a meal; they would not distinguish between a seal and a man," Shackleton noted.

A soccer game on the ice during a "holdup," waiting for a lead to open so the ship could continue.

A huge iceberg observed from the ship, January 16, 1915.

On one occasion, when *Endurance* was moored to a floe, the crew hauled out the motor sledge. Orde-Lees, the motor expert, got the machine going, and Marston pretended it was an ice cream wagon. Several sailors did imitations of Cockney boys begging for a treat as Marston hammed it up as an ice cream vendor. When the kidding was done, however, the men gave the motor sledge a test run. On the uneven surface of the ice, the machine turned out to be awkward and impractical, and plans to use it were abandoned.

As the days went on, *Endurance* crept forward through leads that closed in behind her. Open water was becoming harder and harder to find: a shifting mass of ice stretched from one horizon to the next.

Two and a half weeks into the new year, Hurley wrote in his diary, "It is now seven weeks since we first entered the pack ice, and since then it has been almost an incessant battle." The weather was not improving, and the ice showed no signs of opening. On the next day, January 19, the fist of the Antarctic closed around the ship: *Endurance* was surrounded by ice pack, with no open water in sight. They had sailed 12,000 miles from London. They had picked their way through 1,000 miles of ice pack. Now they were less than 100 miles from the continent itself, but *Endurance* would never reach it.

The sea is frozen into an impenetrable barrier of crushed floes, January 1915.

WINTER ON THE PACK

The pack had closed around *Endurance*. In the words of Orde-Lees, they were stuck "like an almond in the middle of a chocolate bar." With the ship locked in the ice, there really wasn't much for the crew to do. The fo'c'sle hands, the sailors whose job it was to run the ship, had no sailing to do. Worsley had no captaining to do.

But the rest of the men found ways to keep busy. Hurley climbed into the frozen rigging and took scores of photographs, amazing everyone with his fearlessness and yelling outrageous Australian curses, just for fun. Green's job in the galley was one that never varied, no matter what, and he had the stowaway, Blackborrow, to help him. The crew needed to eat, whether the ship was moving or not.

The scientists on board kept up with their experiments, such as they were. Reginald James, the physicist, tinkered with the ship's primitive radio. It was only a receiver, so they could not send news of their predicament, and even under the best conditions the radio was barely capable of picking up the monthly signal from the Falkland Islands. But that never did come through, even after James rigged up an extra length of antenna wire. Boreholes were drilled through the ice for soundings and water samples. Some of the men tried to create some excitement for the biologist, Robert Clark, by putting some pieces of cooked spaghetti into one of his specimen bottles of ocean water. The closemouthed Scottish scientist never mentioned the incident.

Hussey continued to take meteorological readings as the summer began to fade. On February 17, the sun dipped below the horizon at midnight for the first time. The fall was approaching, and winter was rushing in right behind it.

As for Shackleton, the Boss feared that the Imperial Trans-Antarctic Expedition was fated to spend the winter on the ship. There was almost no hope of crossing the continent this year. Making the best of things, he took apart a walking stick made of whalebone discs threaded on a metal rod, and used those as poker chips. Card playing became a regular routine.

Not that Shackleton had completely given up hope of escaping from the

Frank Hurley, taking photos from high in the rigging, "stands bare and hair waving in the wind, where we are gloved and helmeted; he snaps his snap or winds his handle, turning out curses of delight and pictures of Life by the fathom," reported Worsley.

icy prison. The engines were kept stoked, and watches were set to scan the horizon for any open leads of water. If there was any chance of breaking free, the Boss wanted to be ready for it, and he was burning half a ton of coal a day to keep the engines fired. But by March 16, winter on the ice seemed inevitable. Shackleton ordered the fires to be burned down. The men all knew what that meant: they were stuck until the ice broke up in the spring. They were all confident that their Norwegian-built ship, with her thick hull, could withstand being locked in the ice. Shackleton's only serious concern at that point was that the ship would drift far off course with the moving ice pack, causing even more delay. There was nothing to do but make the best of it—and pray they didn't die of sheer boredom.

There was hunting to be done, of course. Now that the trip was delayed by a minimum of several months, the ship's stores had to be supplemented with fresh meat. In February and early March, there had been plenty of life on the ice: there were seals and penguins in every direction. By late March and early

Charles Green, the ship's cook, carving up a seal for meat on board *Endurance*. The doctors on board guessed correctly that seal meat is antiscorbutic (prevents scurvy) and encouraged everyone to eat it as often as possible.

Hubert Hudson holds two emperor penguin chicks. Penguins have no land predators and are not afraid of people, making them easy to catch.

April, game was growing scarcer as the animals migrated north, fleeing the onset of Antarctic winter. Daily hunting parties brought in a large store of meat and blubber for the bitter cold ahead. It was pitifully easy to kill the seals: they had no fear of anything on land, and the men could ski or walk up to the trusting animals and club them to death. Worsley manned the crow's-nest with binoculars, a megaphone, and a flag, searching the ice pack for seals and then shouting and pointing out the seals to the hunters. At the same time, he kept a lookout for killer whales, which nosed up through cracks in the ice.

In order to make the ship's food stores last as long as possible, Shackleton was determined to feed the crew on seal meat, but not everyone approved of the plan. There was some grumbling about seal being fit only for dogs, but the men soon got used to it, especially when it was served as a succulent roast with onions and potatoes.

The hunters brought the big seals back to the ship on dogsleds. Without question, the dogs were the most dependable source of entertainment. Many of them lived in kennels built on deck by dour old McNeish, the carpenter. But just for fun, some of the men also constructed "dogloos" on the ice beside *Endurance*. The dogloo walls were made from blocks of ice, and the roofs were frozen boards of sealskin with snow piled on top. As the weeks went on, the men began to embellish the dogloos into architectural fantasies, adding church spires, minarets, porches, and domes. In spite of the grand accommodations,

Some of the "dogloos."

Frank Wild with two of the dogs from his team. Many of the expedition's dogs were purchased with funds raised by English schools and were named in honor of their sponsors—Harrow, Rugby, and so forth. Other dogs had names such as Shakespeare, Sallie, Wellington, Nelson, Surly, Amundsen, and Sailor.

many of the dogs preferred to sleep outside their houses in the snow. Dog Town, beside the ship, was a noisy center of activity in the middle of a frozen sea, littered with seal bones and dog droppings.

There were six dog teams for the overland journey to be made once *Endurance* got under way again. The drivers were: James McIlroy and Alexander Macklin, the two doctors; Frank Hurley, the photographer; Frank Wild, Shackleton's loyal second-in-command; Tom Crean, the Antarctic veteran; and George Marston, the expedition artist. The six drivers were ferocious in competition with each other, and when Hurley began to boast of having the fastest team, there was nothing to do but hold a race.

On June 15, all hands turned out for the great Antarctic Dog Derby, held on a course called Epsom Downs after the famous racetrack in England.

Dog teams leaving *Endurance*. The teams were harnessed up for training every other day—often wild rides when the half-wolf dogs would tear off in pursuit of penguins.

Betting with chocolate and cigarettes was heavy until someone broke out some gold sovereigns, and then the wagering turned downright feverish. The frenzied yelping and barking of the dogs was brassy in the frozen air. Nearby, a band of penguins, like an audience of formally dressed opera-goers, observed the proceedings. When the starter's gun was fired, the 910-pound sleds were off into the noon twilight on a 700-yard course, with loud shouts of "Mush!"

"Gee!" and "Haw!" from the drivers. As the aurora australis flickered overhead, Wild came in a dog's whisker ahead of Hurley, with a time of two minutes and nine seconds. Groans of dismay and yells of triumph accompanied the exchange of loot.

And it wasn't only among the men that the competition was so hot. In spite of their regular sledging practice and exercise, the dogs themselves were still semi-wild beasts, and dogfights broke out constantly. Bites to dogs and men were common. (Dr. Macklin developed a unique style of breaking up these fights: he simply punched the fighters in the head with his heavy, mittened fist. One or two blows were generally enough to send the fighters yelping into their dogloos.) If the dogs spotted a penguin while on a sledging run, they would chase after it in spite of furious yells from the driver. The waddling penguins didn't stand a chance against the dogs.

Under Shackleton's leadership, fighting never broke out among the men, even though they weren't exactly cut out to be buddies. The fo'c'sle hands were worlds apart from the university scientists, for instance. Many of the personalities of the men wouldn't have meshed even under the best circumstances, let alone cooped up on a ship with nothing to do and nowhere to go.

The men couldn't go anywhere, but in fact the ship was moving. Ever since becoming stuck in the ice, the ship had been steadily drifting north with the pack. The whole ice pack was moving in a clockwise direction, sweeping west and north with the current, up along the Antarctic Peninsula. Whenever Worsley could get a good sighting from the sun or the stars, he calculated the ship's position on the charts: they were making steady progress toward the north, and they all knew that eventually the pack would break up as it reached warmer waters. If they could just be patient, they knew they'd get out of this jam.

The Boss found ways of maintaining a routine in order to keep the crew from going crazy with cabin fever. Each week, every member of the crew, including dogs, was weighed and measured, to see that no one was losing weight—or eating too much. One night, surveying the bearded, shaggy castaways around him, Shackleton ordered haircuts for all. Worsley described the event: "Rickinson gloatingly seizes the clippers and plies them till not a vestige

Captain Frank Worsley (left) and Reginald James, the physicist, take astronomical sights at night to calculate the ship's position.

The haircutting tournament provided a break from the routine—and lots of laughs.

of hair longer than a bristle is left, and his victim looks like one of the Roman Emperors. . . .We all get clipped to a man and look like a group of convicts. The amateur barber seizes his victim with the air of a man about to do a mighty deed. He brandishes the clippers aloft, they descend and a yell of protest arises from the unfortunate object of his attentions. . . . All now look so irresistably quaint, comical, or criminal that the camera is called in to perpetuate this evening and to cure us, where necessary, of conceit of our personal appearances."

Card playing, guessing games, impersonations, listening to gramophone records, slide lectures, reading aloud—the men found ways of entertaining themselves and keeping their thoughts occupied in the long, dark winter months. Worsley gave a lecture on New Zealand and taught several volunteers the Maori war dance, the *haka*. There was a singing contest to determine the worst singer, and the votes overwhelmingly went to the Boss. They even held mock trials, such as the one where Worsley was accused of stealing a trouser

Midwinter dinner,
June 22, 1915.

button from the offering plate of a Presbyterian church. The skipper was found guilty, of course, much to the delight of the fo'c'sle hands. Arguments arose between the FAFs, the Fresh Air Friends, who wanted a hatch open, and the FUGs, the Fetid Undergrounds, who argued against letting out the heat. On June 18, Dr. McIlroy suddenly "discovered" that he had brought his dice along, and betting with the "rattlers" became a popular game. Every Saturday night in "the Ritz," as the common room of the ship was known, a ration of grog was issued to all hands. The toast, as always, was "To our sweethearts and wives—may they never meet!"

Shackleton made sure that the ship's routine was always followed. Breakfast, which usually consisted of porridge, cocoa or tea, bread, butter, and jam, was served at nine in the morning. Lunch of soup, bread and jam, and cocoa was at 1:00 P.M., tea was at 4:00 P.M., and dinner, the most substantial meal of the day, was at 6:00 P.M. In between meals there were ship's chores to do, such as cleaning the decks and common rooms, bringing ice on board to

Feeding the dogs in Dog Town in the dark of winter, June 3, 1915. The dogs were fed one pound of raw meat daily. Dr. Macklin described the routine: "At 5:00 P.M. there is a shout of 'Dog Wallahs,' followed by terrific barking by the dogs. It is feeding time . . . Often there is fighting, and the driver has to freely use his whip, or feet, or fists, to prevent their damaging each other, for when these animals get to grips they show no mercy to each other."

melt into drinking water, or rubbing the eye sprouts off of the two tons of potatoes stored in the hold.

Some of the men looked for any chance to leave their close quarters, in
spite of the bitter cold. Orde-Lees found a bicycle in the hold of the ship and
practiced trick riding on the ice around *Endurance*. He also took long rides in
the darkness until the day he got lost and had to be rescued. Shackleton told
Orde-Lees in no uncertain terms that his bike-riding days were over. Hurley
took advantage of the light whenever possible to take photographs out on the
ice. No matter how many odd jobs or errands the crew dreamed up, however,

one fact remained: there was really nothing to do on the frozen ship but wait, wait, wait.

Some of the dogs had begun ailing, and this caused a great deal of anxiety for their drivers. After fourteen dogs had died, Drs. Macklin and McIlroy performed autopsies and discovered that many of the dogs had worms; the ship's stores did not include the proper medication. Several litters of puppies promised to bring the number of dogs back up, however, and the men made pets of the new pups, carrying them in their pockets and taking them aboard as passengers on sled runs. Tom Crean made a miniature sled for his puppies, and Worsley described their first attempt at pulling. "Crean put his 4 pups in harness for the first time . . . their howls of terror resound for miles around . . . they pursue a devious and uncertain course . . . and they flounder and puff and pant along through the snow until to their joy they are headed for the ship and for a few minutes drag the hated sledge as fast as a dog team." The men were becoming very attached to their dogs, making straw mattresses for the dogloos, saving special treats for their favorites, and even crawling into the dogloos on occasion to share the dogs' warmth. The puppies were kept on board the ship, where they occasionally got loose and ransacked the stores. Many nights, the dog teams set up a wolf pack howl, sending their lonesome cries up toward an aurora australis that was bright enough to cast shadows on the endless field of ice.

Cabin fever reached its peak on Midwinter's Day, June 22, when the crew celebrated with a raucous party. There were mock lectures and sermons, and then Kerr, the second engineer, made an entrance dressed as a tramp and began singing a ridiculous rendition of "Spagoni the Toreador." He started out too high, and Hussey, who was accompanying him on the banjo, kept hissing, "Lower! Lower!" Next, Marston took the stage dressed as a country bumpkin to sing "Widdecombe Fair." Some of the men played a "Discord Fantasia" on homemade instruments, setting the dogs outside howling. At midnight, Green served up a snack of fried bread and onions, which everyone dug into eagerly.

Then Frank Wild tapped the embers from his pipe and stood up to recite "The Wreck of the Hesperus," by Henry Wadsworth Longfellow. The Ritz grew solemn and still as he recited the mournful shipwreck saga and the wind

The crew dressed in costume for a variety show, Midwinter's Day, June 22, 1915. In the days before movies and television, theatricals were a popular form of entertainment, and no ship would have set sail for a long voyage without costumes and props. The crewman on the left in "blackface" illustrates a form of racial slur common to the era which no one today would tolerate.

outside shrieked in the frozen rigging. There were no more jokes. The party ended with a toast and everyone singing "God Save the King." The Antarctic winter was half over when the men finally retired to their cabins and bunks.

Outside in the darkness, the endless mass of pack ice was grinding against itself like a restless giant breaking mountains in its sleep.

PRESSURE

From July 14 through 16, a blizzard pounded the ship with gale force winds. As the temperature dropped to thirty-four degrees below zero, the Boss ordered the team drivers to feed their dogs half a pound of lard each to keep them from freezing—and no man was allowed to leave *Endurance* except to go to Dog Town, where wires were rigged up so the men could grope their way back to the safety of the ship. On board the men huddled around the stove with their books and their pipes, listening to the wind howl through the stays and yardarms, and hearing the unmistakable creak of the ship's timbers as ice pressed against the sides of the ship. Shackleton confided in his diary, "It would be a relief to be able to make some effort on our own behalf; but we can do nothing until the ice releases our ship. In the meantime the pressure continues, and it is hard to foresee the outcome."

For the first time, Shackleton began to voice his doubts about the future of the expedition. In the privacy of his cabin, he and Worsley discussed their dilemma.

"If the *Endurance* does have to, well, get left behind, we will manage, somehow," Worsley said, listening to the howling of the gales outside.

"We shall hang on as long as we can," the Boss replied. "It is hard enough on the men as it is. Without a ship in which to shelter from these blizzards, and in this continuous cold—" He broke off to pace the cabin, and nothing more was said for a time. The wind shrieked again, and the light flickered in a draft.

When the blizzard subsided, a scene of destruction stretched from one ice-white horizon to the other. What had once been a fairly smooth plain was now broken and fractured. Enormous slabs of ice jutted out of the pack at all angles. The wind howled around each mound and hillock and floe, piling up enormous drifts of snow. The garbage dumps had been blown clear of snow and stood out stark and ugly against the white.

But worse, the jumble of ice that stretched for hundreds of miles in every direction gave the wind a grip on the ice pack. As the winds built up speed across the tumbled floes, the frozen sea began to shift and creak and press against itself. On *Endurance,* the ship's timbers began to complain. Loudly.

Hurley's most famous photograph of *Endurance* looks like a negative, but isn't. The ship is completely coated with frost, turning it white, and the winter night is totally black. He took this photograph on the night of August 27, 1915. It required twenty flashes to secure the image on film. "Half blinded after the successive flashes, I lost my bearings amongst hummocks, bumping shins against all points and stumbling into deep snowdrifts," said Hurley.

"Mighty blocks of ice, gripped between meeting floes, rose slowly until they jumped like cherrystones squeezed between thumb and finger," Shackleton wrote.

"The noise was very loud, like an enormous train with squeaky axles being shunted with much bumping and clattering," added Worsley.

Day and night, the men listened to their sturdy ship resist the pressure of the ice. On July 26, the men cheered the return of "Old Jamaica," sailors' slang for the sun. Even its brief appearance raised spirits a little, and by August 1 the pressure on the ship's sides relaxed. The men congratulated one another and praised the ship for withstanding the ice. As August passed in peace and quiet, spirits rose even higher: spring was on the way. Soon the ship would be free, and their journey could continue. All the dogs were brought back on board, in case Dog Town was destroyed by the shifting ice.

But at ten o'clock at night on August 31, the pressure resumed, and the ship began creaking and groaning and trembling like an animal in pain, keeping the men on edge for three days before letting up. September teased them with agonizing on-again, off-again attacks against the ship. Often, it seemed, the pressure

One of the weekly "gramophone evenings" held in "the Ritz"—the common room of *Endurance.*

coincided with their "gramophone evenings," and some of the more superstitious members of the crew began to think the music caused the pressure. The gramophone was banned to save argument. An increase in plankton in the water drawn from the boreholes around the ship—a sure sign of approaching spring—didn't ward off the suspense that all the men now felt. The temperature was rising, the sun was shining longer and longer each day, but *Endurance* wasn't free yet.

Worsley noted in his diary on September 22, the first day of the Antarctic spring, "We seem to be utterly abandoned by animal life, and it will be hard with the dogs if we do not get a few penguins soon." The dogs were shedding their winter coats, whining and restless to be off the ship again, and growing hungrier every day.

The afternoon of September 30 brought an enormous ice floe bearing down on the ship from the port side. The floe, which Worsley estimated at

As the wind increased, it gained a grip on the broken ice and began driving it relentlessly against the ship. "All hands is standing bye, we had a slight shock last . . . there was a noise under the bottom aft the same as if the ice had broken up . . . the Boss thinks it was a whale but I thinks different," wrote McNeish in his diary.

possibly a million tons, pressed so hard against *Endurance* that her beams began to buckle and her foremast jerked and shook like a cornstalk in the wind. The attack lasted an hour, leaving the men stunned. In a daze they bent to retrieve the objects shaken from their perches—books, tools, charts, pots and pans, boxes of tea and tins of tobacco, microscopes, clocks, and diaries—and gaped at the bent and buckled decks.

For the next two weeks, the men felt as though they were holding their breath. They hardly dared hope they had seen the last of the pressure attacks. The pack was still drifting steadily northward, carrying *Endurance* with it. The sun was shining almost around the clock, and the temperature had finally climbed above zero. And then on October 18, a misty, gray day, the ice began pressing in again on both sides of the ship.

The ship began to rise to the pressure that was squeezing it up and out of

The pressure grew stronger, forcing the ship onto its side, when a massive floe rammed against it on October 19, 1915. "We have sprung a leak I am working all night trying to stop it the pressure is getting worse," McNeish wrote.

the ice. Suddenly, *Endurance* rolled over onto the port side, and everything that wasn't nailed down slid, slithered, and crashed against the bulwark. Dogs and men all went head over heels in a mass of howling confusion. Some of the men prepared to jump as the ship leaned onto its side, but *Endurance* came to rest at an angle of thirty degrees to port. The pressure stopped again, and the Boss ordered the men to restore order to the jumbled ship. The crew ate dinner that night propped up against the decks like men seated in a grandstand, with their plates in their laps. At eight o'clock, the ship suddenly righted itself again and floated free. *Endurance* had survived another attack.

The next day, the men studied the narrow lead of open water they found themselves in. A killer whale surfaced beside the ship, its black sides glistening and its white patches tinged a dirty yellow by algae. The animal paraded alongside them for some time before disappearing again. Everything was in readiness for breaking free of the ice. The engines were fired, and sea watches were set as the crew waited for a sizable lead that would take them out of the ice pack. Members of the crew began to talk about the future, of what they would do when they returned home. Reginald James, the physicist, declared that once he got back to Cambridge University he never wanted to see another scrap of ice for the rest of his life. He wasn't the only one to feel that way.

But no navigable leads formed. Days passed, and still *Endurance* and her crew waited in readiness. To their dismay the pressure began again on October 24, and it began so strong and so steady that there could be no doubt: the ship was in for it. The crew had seen pressure before, but none of it compared with what they were seeing now. The whole pack, for as far as the eye could see, was churning and heaving and shuddering. Bergs and floes larger than the ship rose up and tumbled over like children's toys. Icebergs plowed through the pack. Dr. Macklin felt he was watching "something colossal, something in nature too big to grasp."

Endurance was pinned on all sides by this immense upheaval. As floes pressed against her, leaks sprang in the hold. Planks began twisting out of place. Amid the sounds of tortured wood were the howls and whines of the dogs. In the boiler room, the men took turns manning the pumps to keep the water out, but they knew they were toiling for nothing. In a desperate

Endurance slowly but surely being consumed by the ice. McNeish's diary continues: "*Endurance* is going to pieces fast . . . the stern post broke . . . and then the keel was torn out of her then she filled rapidly."

attempt to keep the pressure off the ship, Shackleton ordered some of the men over the side to hack away at the floes, with the axes, and picks. All night long they rotated in shifts from the pumps, to the axes, and back again.

And now the Boss directed the lifeboats, equipment, and stores to be transferred onto the ice beside *Endurance*. In the evening of October 25, a troop of eight emperor penguins waddled out of the fog and stood looking at the embattled ship. They tipped their heads up and began hooting dismally. Although all the men had seen emperor penguins before, none of them had ever heard the birds utter a sound. Now that the emperors were wailing at the ship, it sounded to everyone's ears like a dirge.

"Do you hear that?" asked Thomas McLeod, one of the sailors. "We'll none of us get back to our homes again."

"You won't get home if you stand there gaping!" Wild snapped. "Get the dogs off."

Shackleton turned away and ordered the men to resume their backbreaking, futile work. "It was a sickening sensation to feel the decks breaking up under one's feet, the great beams bending and then snapping with a noise like heavy gun-fire," he wrote later in his diary. The ship was being crushed like a nut, and Shackleton knew there was nothing he could do to stop it.

All that night and the next day the pressure continued without letup. The sternpost was ripped away. The keel was sheared off. The decks began to buckle, and thick beams snapped like twigs. As water rushed forward it weighed down the bow, and the men pumped with every last shred of their failing strength.

But by five o'clock on October 27, Shackleton told them to stop pumping. It was obvious there was no point in going on. The ship could endure no more. In a calm voice he ordered the men over the side. Wild picked his way carefully over the quaking deck and found William Bakewell and Walter How asleep from exhaustion. He shook them awake.

"She's going, boys. I think it's time to get off."

Shackleton had the flag raised one last time on the battered mast, which brought a weary cheer from the men, and then began overseeing the evacuation.

"I brought your banjo ashore," Shackleton said to Hussey. "Look after it.

We shall need it. Then, as Orde-Lees prepared to abandon the ship, the Boss said to him, "We've got it in the neck all right this time, haven't we?"

"Well, no," Orde-Lees ventured. "You wouldn't have had anything to write a book about if it hadn't been for this."

"By Jove, I'm not so sure you aren't right," Shackleton replied, and the two men laughed together.

Then they went over the side, leaving *Endurance* to die in the grip of the ice.

THE FACE OF THE DEEP IS FROZEN

The Antarctic contains ninety percent of the world's snow and ice, and there are more than eighty kinds of it. There's brash ice, pancake ice, bullet ice, green ice, frazil, nilas, breccia, shuga, slush ice, rotten ice, pressure ice, grease ice, ice dust, shorefast ice, ice flowers, ice haycocks, ice saddles, floes, calf bergs, growlers, and sastrugi, to name just a few. And when it comes to icebergs, there are whole family trees to study. In the family of tabular bergs, there are domed, horizontal, blocky, tilted, and uneven bergs; in the tribe of rounded bergs, there are subrounded, well-rounded, and rounded bergs; and when it comes to irregular bergs, there are tabular remnant, pinnacled, pyramidal, drydock, castellate, jagged, slab, and roof bergs.

Much of the ice on the continent of Antarctica is actually a form of consolidated snow called firn. As snow accumulates, it begins to compact, forcing out the air between the snowflakes. Eventually, all the air is squeezed out, and the snow is a dense, heavy ice. This compression also makes much of the ice blue.

These masses of ice form glaciers that reach the edge of the continent, where every year 5,000 to 10,000 icebergs "calve," or break off, from the ice sheets into the surrounding ocean. Many icebergs are so large that they create their own weather systems. The largest iceberg ever recorded was one the size of Belgium (close to 12,000 square miles), spotted in 1956, and the most northerly iceberg reached twenty-six degrees south latitude in the Atlantic Ocean, in 1894. This is the latitude of Rio de Janeiro, in Brazil, just south of the Tropic of Capricorn. As the icebergs drift, the seawater erodes them from below, until the berg abruptly topples over and continues its journey upside down. The erosion continues until the berg flips again, and then again, and eventually it is eroded and melted away.

As the icebergs calve from the glaciers on the continent, they bring with them mineral deposits scraped up from the ground, and release these nutrients into the water. As they melt, the bergs also release atmospheric nutrients that have been trapped in the ice for centuries. It is this steady deposit of nutrients

Frank Wild surveys the wreckage of *Endurance*.

from icebergs that makes the waters of the Southern Ocean so rich and full of life.

Of course, the ocean around the continent also turns to ice. Salt water freezes at a lower temperature than fresh water, around twenty-seven degrees Fahrenheit, depending on the concentration of salt and other minerals. As the water on the surface cools, it begins to condense, and individual ice crystals act as seeds, causing the water to congeal around them, squeezing the salt out into the water below. On the surface, the water seems to stiffen and turn greasy. This layer of thick, flexible ice is called nilas. If the nilas is disturbed by wind, the ice forms rounded discs called pancakes, which look something like white lily pads with their edges turned up. As the air temperature drops and the water continues to freeze, the pancakes mass together and harden into a single sheet, or ice field. Because the water forces out salt as it freezes, the water below the ice field is saturated with salt and minerals, and the ice itself is clean enough to melt into drinking water.

This process of turning seawater into drinking water is important: it means that a shipwreck on the frozen sea does not *necessarily* mean certain death.

When the exhausted crew of *Endurance* gave up the battle against the pressure and abandoned the ship, the ice field around her was not a sight to inspire confidence. The ship itself was a mess of snapped rigging and broken spars. Beside her on the ice was Dump Camp, a junk pile of most of the stores and equipment the men had. The dogs milled around, straining at their tethers, snapping and snarling at one another. The crew staggered like dead men, utterly beaten from their labors, trying to pitch tents so they could crawl in to sleep. There were only eighteen sleeping bags, originally meant for the overland journey, and the men drew straws to see who would get them. The rest of the men had to make do with wool blankets. Tom Crean was suffering from snow blindness (a temporary condition that often affects polar travelers when they are exposed to the glare of sunlight on snow); he had to be helped into a tent. That night, the ice beneath the tents quivered as whales rubbed up against it from below.

"Though we have been compelled to abandon the ship, which is crushed beyond all hope of ever being righted, we are alive and well, and we have stores and equipment for the task that lies before us. The task is to reach land with all the members of the expedition," Shackleton wrote in his diary the next morning.

There were precious few options available to the Boss. Already the ship had drifted 1,000 miles north and west with the pack ice. The tip of South America was more than 2,000 miles away, and there was no way of reaching it on foot. They had ample food, guns, matches, and dogs. But, after all, they were in the Antarctic, not Hyde Park in London. The circumstances were dire, to say the least.

After a quiet conference with Wild, Shackleton announced his plan to the crew: they would march across the frozen sea with two of the three lifeboats to Paulet Island, 346 miles to the northwest. To the best of Shackleton's knowledge, there was a cache of stores in a hut on Paulet Island from a 1902 Swedish expedition. What they would do once they reached this destination was not specified: it was enough to have a goal. He would plan the next step when they got there. But 346 miles is more than the distance between Boston and New York City, almost as far as from Los Angeles to San Francisco, about the entire width of Iowa. They would have to walk the whole way, hauling their gear and the two boats. The men knew they were doomed without the boats; eventually they would reach open water. They would need the boats, no matter how burdensome they were to drag over the ice. Shackleton gave the men a couple of days' rest. October 30 was the appointed day of departure.

In the meantime, there was much to get ready. Mrs. Chippy, the carpenter's cat, had to be shot, because without the protection of the ship the dogs would have eaten him. The youngest of the puppies, who were too small to pull with a team, also had to be killed. While McNeish and McLeod began fitting the lifeboats onto sledges, the rest of the crew began sorting their equipment. The men were given a two-pound limit on personal gear, which allowed them to keep only the items that were essential for survival—although the Boss did allow them to keep their diaries and their tobacco, and the doctors were allowed their medical supplies. In a dramatic gesture, Shackleton took his gold cigarette case and a handful of gold coins from his pocket and dropped them on the snow. Gold was useless for the task ahead.

He then opened the Bible inscribed to him by Queen Alexandra and ripped out a page from the Book of Job:

> Out of whose womb came the ice?
> And the hoary frost of Heaven, who hath gendered it?
> The waters are hid as with a stone,
> And the face of the deep is frozen.

Then he folded the page into a pocket and dropped the heavy Bible on the cigarette case and gold coins, showing the crew the route they must take. If they wanted to survive, they must travel light, harden their hearts against sentimental keepsakes, and trust that they could make do with the bare bones of equipment. Shackleton the improviser believed that it was foolish to burden themselves with equipment for *every* possible emergency. As the day wore on, the pile of discards grew. Extra clothes, books, scientific instruments and specimens, chess sets, flags, lanterns, tools, sewing kits, lucky talismans, razors, barometers, combs, scissors, playing cards, dishes, silverware, photographs—each man added to the heap. Some of the men saved leather suitcases to use for boot repairs later on. Hussey kept his toothbrush, and Shackleton ordered him to keep the banjo, because they would need the comfort of music in the hard months ahead. Each man kept a spoon and a knife.

The journey was ready to begin at 2:00 P.M. on October 30 under heavy gray skies. It had already snowed on and off during the day, and it threatened to continue. That didn't pose much of a problem, but the road ahead did. If they only had to trek across 346 miles of flat ice field, the journey would have been bearable. But stretching ahead of them into the white horizon was a scene of utter devastation and chaos. It was as if a giant hand had smashed down onto the frozen face of the deep and broken it into a million shards. Jagged floes tilted up at all angles. Pressure ridges reared up like wrinkles in a huge white blanket. If the sea had been frozen at the height of a tempest, and every storm-tossed wave locked into place, the scene could not have been more jumbled and uneven. There were 346 miles of *that* to cross—assuming the drift of the pack didn't change course and carry them helplessly in another direction.

The crew drags the *James Caird,* fitted with sled runners, over the ice to their next camp. Even on smooth ice this was a difficult task. Once the ice became broken and jumbled it became impossible.

On the lead sled went Shackleton, Wordie, Hussey, and Hudson, looking for the best route among the pressure ridges and tumbled ice floes. They were equipped with shovels, picks, and axes to chop a path through the chaos of ice. Behind them came the other dog teams pulling sleds that were each loaded with 900 pounds of stores and gear.

Bringing up the rear was the remainder of the crew pulling the boats on sledge runners. Loaded with food and equipment, the boats weighed in at more than a ton apiece. Fifteen men in harness dragged one boat at a time across the wet snow and over the ice, stopping every quarter mile to rest, before going back to haul the second boat forward. Shackleton was in constant anxiety over continuing pressure in the ice. If a crack opened up between one team and another, the result could be disastrous. So he kept the men and sleds and boats close together, relaying forward one agonizing quarter mile at a time. Frequently, one of the dog teams had to be unharnessed from its sled and then hitched to a lifeboat to help the men drag it up and over a hummock or ridge.

After two hours of backbreaking labor, hauling the boats through wet, heavy snow, detouring around piles of broken floe, they were only one mile from *Endurance*. Soaked, and numb with fatigue, the men swallowed a hasty dinner and fell into their tents. It began to snow during the night. When the men resumed their burdens the next day, they had a new layer of heavy, wet slush to trudge through, and more wet snow was falling steadily. After another three hours and only an additional three quarters of a mile, the Boss called a halt. He and Worsley were worried about damaging the boats as they knocked their way across the ice. They were getting nowhere.

At the moment they were on a very large, level floe, more than a half a mile in diameter. There wasn't another good, solid, flat floe in sight, and Shackleton felt they could not do better for a camping place. The men pitched their tents on the wet snow and crawled into their sleeping bags. Shackleton anxiously scouted ahead and found it impossible to advance.

Next morning, he announced that they would stay where they were and let the drifting pack carry them northward into a better position to make for Paulet Island. There was no alternative. Shackleton told Green to start adding large chunks of blubber to the crew's food. The thick seal fat that kept the animals warm would provide valuable calories in the men's diets and keep them from freezing. It was time to get used to it.

OCEAN CAMP

Over the next few days, the men made several trips back to Dump Camp and the wrecked ship to salvage everything they could, including the third lifeboat. More precious foodstores—cases of nuts, boxes of sugar, crates of barley, flour, and jam—were sledged back to the new camp, dubbed Ocean Camp by the men. In all, they rescued more than three tons of food.

McNeish pried nails from *Endurance*'s distorted decking and made a stockpile of scrap lumber, including the lumber that had been meant for the expedition's winter hut. Other men tried to retrieve some of their own personal items abandoned in the rush, particularly books. They knew they would have a lot of time on their hands and very little to do.

How and Bakewell waded through the icy water that flooded the belowdecks cabins and brought out an important treasure from the darkroom: Frank Hurley's box of glass photographic plates. There were more than 400 of them, documenting the voyage and ordeal of *Endurance*, but they weighed far too much to save all of them. Hurley was faced with the heartbreaking task of selecting which few to keep. He and Shackleton sat on the snow, picking and choosing among the best pictures, smashing the rejects as they went to keep from changing their minds. In the end, they whittled the number down to 150 photographs. Hurley also kept a Kodak pocket camera and three rolls of film, with which he documented the remainder of the crew's odyssey.

The talented Hurley was also skilled as a metalworker. Using the few tools they saved, he fashioned two camp stoves, one using the ash chute from the ship's boilers, and another, smaller one from the ash bucket. Both of these stoves were stoked with seal blubber and could boil two and a half gallons of water from ice in half an hour. The carpenter took apart the wheelhouse from the ship and rebuilt it at Ocean Camp for a galley, and the larger "hot potato can," as the stove was called, was installed inside. Green set up this new galley and was soon serving up hot stews, tea, and cocoa. The thick, greasy smoke from the blubber stove turned his face black and regularly sent him bursting outside coughing and choking, but he remained cheerful.

At Ocean Camp, the crew still had much of their gear and supplies, including their skis and a Union Jack presented to them by King George of England.

Shackleton had also drafted plans for each man's duty in an emergency. These orders were written up and posted on the tents, and the Boss let it be known that he might at any time give a false alarm as a drill.

It was now November, and although the sixth of the month brought a blizzard, the Antarctic summer was reaching its peak. On November 12, the temperature soared to thirty-five degrees Fahrenheit, and several men took advantage of the warmth to take a wash in the snow. With water so hard to come by and the weather usually so cold, keeping clean was a luxury. As for going to the bathroom, the men had to find a convenient ice hummock to squat behind for privacy. Their floe was soon dirty with blubber soot, dog droppings, sealskins, penguin heads, and other garbage, but the men all adjusted to a new set of standards without complaint. They were alive. What did dirt matter?

The ice pack, with Ocean Camp piggybacking along, made a steady three miles north every day. If the men could be patient, the ice would carry them closer to their destination. All they had to do was wait—just as they had while trapped on the ship—but now they had even less to do and much more discomfort, as well.

Living quarters were cramped. There were five canvas tents to hold the twenty-eight members of the crew. Some of the men were able to fashion wooden floors using scrap lumber, and others used sealskins for ground cloths, but even so, the rising temperatures outside and body heat inside meant that the snow beneath them was constantly melting. The men were soaking wet all the time and had to become ingenious in finding ways to keep their possessions dry. They constructed rickety shelves from packing crates, and hung their gear from tent poles or stored it in empty cans. During the warm days when the men went about their business on the floe, the softening ice frequently gave way underfoot, plunging them into cold water up to their waists.

At first the men were not miserable. The sun shone more than twenty hours a day, and they knew they were on their way north. Optimism remained high. If the pack carried them north fast enough, they could reach the edge of the ice and be able to launch the boats. Frank Worsley pored over his navigational charts, studying possible courses. He plotted courses to Paulet Island, Elephant Island, Clarence Island, even far-off South Georgia Island, where

OCEAN CAMP

57

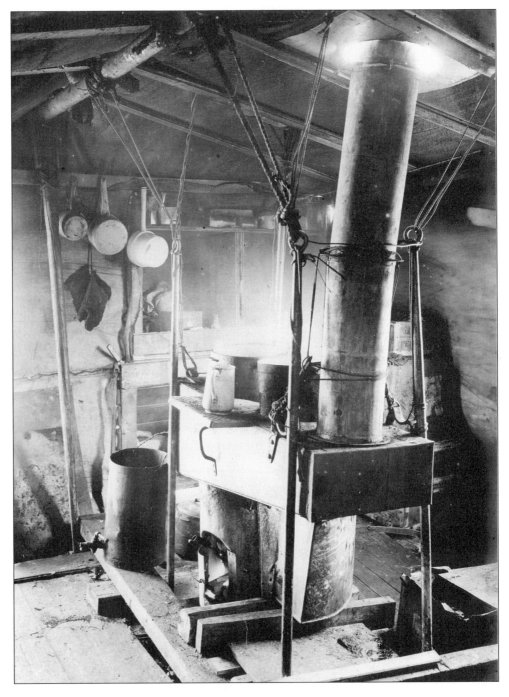

The galley (kitchen) at Ocean Camp, constructed from scrap lumber salvaged from *Endurance*.

they had last set foot on land. Every day when he took his sightings with the sextant and calculated their position, the crew eagerly waited to hear how far they had traveled. Sometimes it was a useless mile to the west or east. Sometimes it was a heartening run dead north. Slowly but surely, they were on their way out of Antarctica's grip.

McNeish busied himself preparing the boats. With scrap lumber from *Endurance* and a small and precious collection of used nails, he began raising the sides of the boats to make them more seaworthy. "I have only a saw, hammer, chisel, and adze, but we are managing alright," he reported in his diary. He filled the seams between the new planks with wool yarn unraveled from a scarf and then caulked them with Marston's oil paints. McNeish had every right to be proud of his ingenuity.

The rest of the men occupied themselves the best they could. Marston continued painting, using his remaining paint and the lids of packing crates for canvases. Others spent their days hunting seals and penguins, which had returned with the warmer weather. One afternoon, Macklin and First Officer Lionel Greenstreet went out in search of seals. Finding a small floe near an open lead, they jumped onto the floe and began paddling around with ski poles like boys on a raft. Shackleton was not amused. He hated unnecessary risks and disapproved of such shenanigans, knowing that leopard seals and killer whales could easily surface inside a lead and make a quick meal of the men.

November 21, 1915, brought an unforgettable evening. Most of the men were lying in their tents reading or playing cards. Shackleton, restless as always, was standing on an ice hill that the men frequently used for a lookout tower. In their tents, the men suddenly heard the Boss cry out, "She's going, boys!"

Struggling out onto the ice, the crew witnessed the last of *Endurance*, a mile and a half away, as her bows went under. Then the ship dived quickly and the ice closed over her with a rush.

"At 5 P.M. she went down by the head: the stern . . . was the last to go under water," Shackleton recorded in his diary that night. "I cannot write about it."

The long-delayed death of their ship sent a wave of sadness and depression over the crew. While she lasted, *Endurance* had been a visible link to the world they once knew. Now they were utterly alone on the sea of ice.

Tempers began to wear thin in the close quarters. From time to time, Shackleton would reassign men to different tents to keep them from getting on each other's nerves. He always found some excuse for these moves besides breaking up quarrels, but always, when he transferred the men, he reminded them that they could survive only by cooperating.

Shackleton couldn't let the men brood for long. With the advance of the spring, their floe was eroding at the edges. Sometimes a whole chunk would break away. In addition, the accumulation of black soot and debris around the camp was soaking up the heat of the sun and warming the floe, turning the surface to slush. On December 1, the Boss decided to move fifty yards to a new, clean site and set up their camp on firmer ice, and on December 5, he declared a holiday in honor of the anniversary of their departure from South Georgia Island.

Meanwhile, the drift of the ice had shifted to the east, taking them farther away from possible landing sites. Shackleton and his most trusted advisers frequently debated their options and kept themselves ready to move. If the ice took them toward the east, they would reach open water with no near landfalls; if it took them west, their chances were better. They knew that they would have to head west over the ice again if their position didn't improve.

Macklin described what a visitor might see if he stumbled upon Ocean Camp at midnight. "He would notice that it was still light, the sun never setting at this time of year in this latitude. He would have to pass a line of dogs tethered in teams to wires secured at one end to their own loaded sledges and at the other to an iron stanchion driven deeply in the snow. The sledge trace is in position and the harnesses all secured in place and ready to be put on the dogs. The sledges are loaded and lashed, and everything ready to be moved at a moment's notice."

For the first three weeks of December, the pack was constantly on the move, but each time it edged toward the east, away from the Antarctic Peninsula and its outlying islands, Shackleton became anxious. Their floe was continuing to decay rapidly, so the Boss made a decision on December 21. They would strike camp again and head west over the ice, trying to narrow the gap between themselves and the islands. They would spend the twenty-second celebrating Christmas, and start for Paulet Island on December 23. It was mid-summer in the Antarctic: the weather from now on would begin to go down-hill.

Shackleton made the holiday a celebration. He allowed the men to eat as much as they desired. "We consumed most of our small remaining stock of lux-uries," he wrote later. "For the last time for eight months we really had as much as we could eat. Anchovies in oil, baked beans, and jugged hare made a glori-ous mixture." They also feasted on ham and sausages, canned milk, biscuits, coffee, pickles, parsnips, and peaches.

Then, on the twenty-third, the men harnessed themselves to the boats again and resumed the backbreaking haul across the ice.

Shackleton and Wild, at left, and the rest of the crew on a mild day at Ocean Camp.

MUTINY

One of the most infamous stories of polar exploration is Sir John Franklin's doomed search for the Northwest Passage. In 1845, Franklin took two Royal Navy ships, *Erebus* and *Terror,* and a crew of 129 into the Arctic to search for a sea route between the North Atlantic and the Pacific. They never returned. Years later, a record of the fateful voyage was discovered among some artifacts in Arctic Canada. Mutiny, insanity, desertion, cannibalism—dreadful things were whispered about the members of the Franklin expedition. More than forty rescue missions were sent from England, at least ten of them financed by Lady Franklin, the leader's widow.

A book about one of Lady Franklin's rescue missions, *The Voyage of the Fox,* was among the nonessential stores and equipment left behind at Ocean Camp. The essentials were now being dragged laboriously over the ice by *Endurance's* crew. Far to their west on the Antarctic Peninsula was Erebus and Terror Gulf, named in honor of the two ships that had navigated the bottom of the world before being lost at the top. Without doubt, Shackleton's men were well versed in stories about the Franklin voyage and well aware of the dangers that faced them as they manhauled two of the boats over the rotting ice toward a very uncertain goal.

Shackleton had hoped by setting out across the ice to enliven the crew and focus their minds on action. Instead, he found himself faced with growing resentment and dissatisfaction. Now that *Endurance* was gone, some of the fo'c'sle hands were grumbling that they were working without pay and were no longer bound to follow Shackleton's orders. In addition, Worsley was constantly fretting about the boats: Shackleton had decided to leave one of them, the *Stancomb Wills,* behind at Ocean Camp. But Worsley knew that cramming the whole crew into the *James Caird* and the *Dudley Docker* once they reached the open ocean would be difficult, if not impossible: the two boats would ride low and heavy in the water, and maneuvering them would take all their skill.

But to drag all three boats—Shackleton knew *that* was impossible. As it was, the men hauling the *Caird* and the *Docker* were sinking up to their knees in slush, and their boots were filling with seven pounds of freezing water with each step. They marched at night, when the surface of the pack was slightly cooler and harder, but even so the labor was horrendous. Again, they relayed one boat at a time in quarter-mile stages, trudging back over their own tracks to bring up the second boat. Often, by the time they reached the second boat, they would find the runners of the sledge frozen onto the ice, and they would have to lunge forward three or four times like exhausted draft horses to snap it free. The dog teams broke the trail as much as possible, but in three days they covered only seven miles. They would certainly have traveled much faster and easier without the boats. But without the boats, they hadn't a chance. They would eventually reach the edge of the pack and have the ocean in front of them. They *had* to take the boats.

On December 27, Shackleton turned back from breaking trail to find that the men hauling the boats were standing idle. Soaked with sweat and seawater, the crew shuffled their feet in the snow, looking anxious and avoiding Shackleton's eyes. Overhead a lone petrel circled, watching the scene. Worsley, angry and exasperated, was in a standoff with a mulish, silent McNeish. The carpenter had decided not to take another step.

Under naval law, a ship's crew is free of obligation when the ship sinks. Their duties are terminated, and their pay ceases. After years at sea McNeish knew his naval law, and he was convinced that *Endurance*'s Ship's Articles were canceled. He wasn't going to follow orders from Worsley or Shackleton or anyone else any longer. He had had enough.

This was the first threat to Shackleton's command, but it was a potentially disastrous one. Chances for survival were slim at best if they all stayed together. But if the crew broke apart and chose their own courses, their chances would dwindle to nothing. At the moment, nobody was siding with McNeish—after all, staying behind was obviously fatal.

But Shackleton knew how close his crew was to falling apart. The fo'c'sle hands, along with McNeish, had begun grumbling about their duties and pay since the ship sank. And some of the university men, who were unused to such a hard life, were so demoralized by the events of the last months that they seemed ready to break down. Once a man sat down on the ice and decided not to continue, it would require force or threats of violence to get him moving again.

Shackleton returned to the sledge that carried the ship's crew list. Paper in hand, in a quiet, steady voice, he read the Ship's Articles, which each man had signed before leaving England. They had been modified slightly from the usual contract:

> All members of the Crew without exception to have interchangeable duties. . . . The Crew agree to conduct themselves in an orderly, faithful, honest, and sober manner, and to be at all times diligent in their respective Duties, and to be obedient to the lawful commands of the said Master . . . whether on board, in boats, or on shore.

Shackleton was the Master, and technically they were now on shore; disobedience to the commands of the Master was legally punishable. The Ship's Articles had not been terminated, and neither had the crew's pay. As the sailors' discontent subsided, Shackleton took McNeish aside and exchanged a few quiet words with him, perhaps reminding him that execution was a legal punishment for mutiny. After a short rest, the men wearily harnessed themselves to the boat once more, and McNeish took his place with the others.

The exhausted band of sleds crept over the ice through another night, covering only two and a half miles. The way grew increasingly difficult. The ice was so thin in some places that the heavy lifeboats cracked the floes and formed leads of seawater. Bergs and broken floes were jumbled together between increasingly large leads of open water. Progress in any direction began to look impossible.

The next day, they retreated to a large, old floe that seemed solid, and there they pitched camp, but they soon discovered it was not as secure as they had hoped. They could not go forward. The way back to Ocean Camp was impassable. The ice was too soft to cross, but there was not enough open water to launch the boats. They moved a short distance again, and then one more time.

At last, they made a new camp. It appeared that they had abandoned

Ocean Camp for no advantage at all. Their new floe was smaller and less stable. They had left behind many of the things they had salvaged from *Endurance,* including the scrap lumber that had made dry floors for their flimsy, canvas tents. They were stuck where they were, and the ice pack was crumbling to pieces beneath them.

On December 31, 1915, Shackleton wrote in his diary: "The last day of the old year: May the new one bring us good fortune, a safe deliverance from this anxious time, and all good things to those we love so far away."

If their loved ones so far away could have seen the crew of *Endurance,* their hearts would have broken. Nothing could have been more pitiful and hopeless than the twenty-eight men marooned on the rotting ice pack nearly 200 miles from the nearest solid land. They called their new home Patience Camp.

PATIENCE, PATIENCE, PATIENCE

On January 1, Orde-Lees was skiing near the edge of the floe when a twelve-foot-long, fanged leopard seal lunged up out of the water and began humping toward him at astonishing speed. With a terrified yell, Orde-Lees stumbled across the ice toward camp. Suddenly, the animal lunged back into the water. As Orde-Lees had reached the opposite side of the floe, the leopard seal burst up out of the water in front of him, jaws agape. Screaming, Orde-Lees turned his skis and headed back. His frantic cries brought Wild out of his tent with a rifle, and Wild immediately dropped to one knee, raised the weapon, and began firing—and cursing furiously at Orde-Lees. The leopard seal now rushed toward Wild, who shot again and again. The animal was only thirty feet away from Wild when it fell at last. The entire crew was breathless.

An attack by a leopard seal was not a great way to begin life in the new camp. Everyone knew they were in worse circumstances than they had been even at Ocean Camp. They had fewer provisions and less equipment with them. The ice was growing so soft they often had to crawl on their hands and knees through saltwater slush, while hungry beasts that looked upon men as a new variety of food cruised through the dark waters just below them.

And although there were seals around for them to hunt, the men grew alarmed when the animals became harder and harder to find. Their food stores were running out. On January 13, Shackleton announced that most of the dogs would have to be killed—the dogs required a seal a day, while the whole crew could survive on one seal for several days. For the time being, the Boss would spare Hurley's, Macklin's, and Greenstreet's teams in order to return to Ocean Camp for supplies when conditions permitted. The other dogs were taken one by one behind a large block of ice and shot.

A gale set in on the fifteenth, and winds of more than seventy miles per hour drove them north for six days. On the twenty-first, Worsley's astronomical observations indicated that they had crossed the Antarctic Circle. Shackleton celebrated the occasion by issuing an extra round of hot Virol, a powdered drink mix, to all hands.

Progress to the north was what they all hoped for, and yet some of the men, especially Worsley and Macklin, remained uneasy about the boats. Worsley had little confidence that they could take to the open ocean in only two boats, and he pestered Shackleton every day about returning to Ocean Camp for the *Stancomb Wills*. On January 22, Worsley climbed a hillock of ice and saw that the gale that had blown them north had also compacted the ice and blown Ocean Camp closer to their position.

Shackleton debated for days. The condition of the pack was miserable for travel, but not likely to get any better. If they were ever to retrieve the third boat, they must do it sooner rather than later. Finally, at the end of the month, he decided to risk a salvage mission. Wild left Patience Camp with eighteen men at one o'clock in the morning of February 1. The rest of the crew waited, some of them crying from restlessness, depression, or anxiety.

According to Hurley, "Ocean Camp presented a forlorn appearance, resembling a deserted Alaskan mining village that had been ransacked by bandits." The men scavenged what they could, loaded the boat, and headed back.

At Patience Camp, Shackleton stood watch. In a new galley made by wrapping canvas around four oars stuck upright in the snow, Green kept the hot potato can stoked. At 11 A.M., Shackleton saw the salvage party returning, and he went out to meet them with a kettle of hot tea. Shortly after noon the *Stancomb Wills* and some of the remaining stores were safely back in camp. With the exception of Macklin's team, the remaining dogs were shot.

Hurley was heartbroken. "I said good-bye to my faithful old leader, Shakespeare, with an aching heart. It seemed like murdering in cold blood a trusty pal, but, alas, there was no alternative. Food was running short and the end was inevitable, for the dogs could not be taken in the boats."

And now there was really nothing left to do but wait. The men suffered from a diet that consisted almost entirely of meat. Constipation and flatulence, or "squeaky gut," as the men called it, made them even more uncomfortable than they already were. With no yeast, the flour they had could not be made into bread, but instead was baked into heavy, unleavened scones. On top of intestinal problems, the wind made the men's eyes water constantly, and their tears would drip down their noses and form a small icicle, which would break

In the frigid air, moisture from the men's breath froze on their whiskers, forming "breath icicles."
Lionel Greenstreet, the first officer, posed for this picture illustrating the effect.

off, tearing a bit of skin at the same time. Dog bites and knife nicks on the men's hands were frequently infected with seal blood, but there were no anti-biotics to treat the inflammation.

When the surface of the floe was firm enough, the men would exercise by marching back and forth, always on the lookout for predatory leopard seals. Some of the men were morbidly convinced that a killer whale would crash upward through their dwindling floe, tossing them all into the water and pick-ing them off one by one. They became obsessed with the wind—its direction, its speed, its temperature. They were all miserable, cold, and completely filthy, since the last of the soap had been saved for Green, who stood all day in the greasy smoke of the blubber stoves. They began calling their forced imprison-ment "The Ice Age."

The games and amusements that had passed the time for them on board *Endurance* were forgotten; no one had the heart for charades or poetry recitals or comic songs. The monotony was punctuated by meals; between meals, they waited for the next. They read and reread their small stock of books. Watches were kept for seals, and if the ice was favorable, a hunting party would go out to kill them. Very often, there were no seals. They ate penguins when they could get them. Twenty penguins, cooked by the fuel of their own skins, was a fair daily average, Hurley said later. Young penguins were tasty enough, much like chicken, but the older penguins were difficult to cut with a knife and almost impossible to chew.

"The worst thing is having to kill time," James wrote in his diary. "It seems such a waste, yet there is nothing else to do."

McNeish wrote, "There is nothing for it but to get in our sleeping bags and smoke away the hunger."

"The water is drip-dripping from the tent roof," Macklin wrote in his diary. "I pray God to give us dry weather soon, for this is misery. I have never seen such depression of spirits as there is in the tent."

The Boss knew how dire their plight was. Almost every night, he shouted himself awake from nightmares in which he pictured one disaster or emergency after another. Would the boats be separated when they took to the ocean? Would he himself be incapacitated? Would Worsley's navigational books be lost? Would they run out of food? One after another, disasters visited his sleep and shook him awake. Then, in the remaining hours of the night, he would form plans for meeting the crises he had dreamed of.

In spite of his anxiety, he tried to keep up the appearance of calm in order to maintain morale. Although tortured by worry, he remained outwardly unperturbed. "He was always cheerful, and gave everyone confidence that we would get out," said Bakewell, oblivious of the Boss's unease.

Shackleton believed that keeping to some pretense of normal routine would calm the men's nerves and settle their fears. Meals were served strictly according to schedule. Watches were rotated regularly. He woke the men by whistle every morning and gave the order to "lash up and stow." For his own sanity, Shackleton played bridge and taught others how to play. He also played exactly four hands of poker with Hurley every afternoon. By the end of ten weeks, he had won imaginary tickets to all the London theaters, boxes of linen handkerchiefs, silk umbrellas, a mirror, and a coveted collector's copy of *Paradise Regained* from Hurley, while Hurley had won from Shackleton a shaving mirror, several top hats, enough walking sticks to equip a regiment, several sets of cuff links, and a library of books, as well as dinner at Claridge's Hotel in London and a box at the opera.

Remain calm. Keep to the normal routines. "Patience. Patience. Patience," the Boss wrote in his diary.

On February 8, one of the men found a twig tangled in some seaweed, and the crew gathered around as the twig was fed to the fire. The scent of burning wood reminded everyone of land so far away, and sunk many of the men into nostalgia and fresh pangs of homesickness.

On February 20, the crew awoke to find that their floe had been invaded by an enormous flock of Adélie penguins migrating north. Each man fell to the task of killing as many as he could. With no natural enemies out of the water, the penguins were easy to catch. Although the birds did not provide much meat, their skins, lined with a thick layer of fat, made a good fuel for the blubber stove. Over the next two days, the crew had brought in more than 600 Adélies. Then the flock moved on, and the ice around Patience Camp was streaked with blood and red penguin guano.

The crew continued to wait. The days dragged slowly on, growing shorter as autumn set in. The weather was gray, rainy, cold, and damp. The ice pack continued its slow, enormous revolution north through the Weddell Sea. When the blubber supply ran alarmingly low, Shackleton reduced the ration of warm drinks to one a day. All their hopes were now pinned on getting safely to the open ocean before the floe they camped on broke into pieces. If the pack disintegrated too soon, they would be unable to launch the boats and maneuver in the jumble of broken and grinding ice, and unable to find a floe large enough to camp on.

"Day passes day with very little or nothing to relieve the monotony," Greenstreet wrote in his diary on March 5. "We take constitutionals round and round the floe but no one can go further as we are to all intents and purposes on an island. There is practically nothing fresh to read and nothing to talk about, all topics being absolutely exhausted. . . . The pack around looks very much as it did four or five months ago and with the low temperature we have been getting at night, i.e., zero and below, the open patches of water get covered with young ice which is neither fit to go over nor would allow the passage of the boats."

It was more than a year since *Endurance* had first become stuck in the ice. Some of the men were dangerously close to believing they would never get out of the ice at all.

On March 9, for the first time since entering the pack, the men felt the swell of the ocean slowly lift the ice under their feet. Around them, the pack was creaking and groaning rhythmically, like the breathing of an immense animal. The open ocean was thirty miles away.

INTO THE BOATS

How did they know where they were? Since the outset of their voyage through featureless ocean and anonymous ice pack, the officers and crew of *Endurance* had been able to track their exact location and chart their zigzagging progress on their maps. This was before the use of radio signals to plot position, before radar, before satellites. They used a few basic instruments, some almanacs, and math.

For centuries, mapmakers, astronomers, and navigators have marked the globe with imaginary lines of latitude, which are parallel to the equator (and are often called parallels), and lines of longitude (also called meridians), great circles that all run through the North and South poles. The meridians are perpendicular to the parallels on the surface of the globe; that is, they meet at right angles, or ninety degrees. When a navigator knows his coordinates—the degree of latitude and degree of longitude he is at—he knows where on the wide, blank ocean he is. But how *does* he know the latitude and longitude?

Astronomers have long known that the celestial bodies—the sun, the moon, the planets, and the stars—follow regular and predictable paths through the heavens, and centuries of patient nighttime observation have produced detailed almanacs listing the daily positions of these bodies. As a navigator moves farther north or south, the height of a star above the horizon changes. Using an instrument called a sextant, the navigator can measure the height of the star above the horizon. Then, by referring to the almanacs and making some calculations, he can determine how far north or south he is: that is his latitude. No matter where on the globe the observer is, an accurate measurement of that star's height, or altitude, and the use of proper almanacs or tables will provide latitude.

Longitude proved to be a harder puzzle to solve. Astronomers have known for centuries that the earth takes twenty-four hours to complete one full rotation—one day. Because a circle (one rotation) is 360 degrees, it is possible to divide 360 by twenty-four to find out how many degrees the earth spins in just one hour. The answer is fifteen degrees. With that information, longitude is within reach—assuming accurate clocks. Imagine a traveler going west with two clocks. After several days, it is no longer noon when the clocks say twelve. So the traveler adjusts the first clock to read twelve when it is noon where he is. The second clock tells a different time, the time at the starting point. If the difference in time is one hour, the traveler knows he has gone fifteen degrees. He can continue to travel as long as he wants, always resetting the first clock at noon, when the sun is at its highest point in the sky. As long as he continues to wind the second clock, and as long as it is accurate, he will know the time difference between his present position and his starting point. He can then convert the difference in time to a distance in degrees.

This makes accurate clocks indispensable on ocean voyages, but it wasn't until the eighteenth century that accurate clocks became a reality. In 1714, the British Parliament offered a prize to the person who could solve the longitude puzzle. Decades later, the prize was awarded to a clockmaker, John Harrison. The mechanism of Harrison's chronometer could withstand the turbulent motion of a ship at sea, defy changes of temperature, and resist the corrosion of salt water and air. His first three models were large, clumsy, heavy instruments, but his final masterpiece was not much larger than a heavy pocket watch. Any captain could take such a timekeeper to sea with him. Harrison had solved the problem of fixing longitude.

By 1914, when *Endurance* set sail from London, dependable and accurate chronometers were every skipper's constant companions. Armed with sextant, chronometers, compass, and nautical tables, Frank Worsley, skipper of *Endurance,* had been able to calculate and plot their every position. He was able to judge the pack's rate of travel by comparing positions from one day to the next. He knew how far they were from the nearest land; he knew when they had crossed the Antarctic Circle; he knew how many miles of forbidding ocean still lay between the crew and their home. Of course, there were many days on the ice when getting a sight from the heavens was impossible. Fog, cloud cover, blizzard conditions, rain, and foul weather of every description often hid the sun and stars from Worsley's sight. But whenever the sun made an appearance, he was sure to take as many readings as he could. The big box chronometers on the ship had been abandoned at Dump Camp, but Worsley had chronometer watches. He periodically checked their accuracy by taking a kind of astronomical reading called an occultation. Most astronomers use the moon or the major planets for their occultations: Worsley used tiny Mercury once, "just for swank," to show he could do it.

Nobody liked to think what might happen if Worsley lost any of his instruments or tables. After Shackleton, they looked to the skipper to get them home. How else would they find their way?

Now, after the initial excitement of the ocean swell, the men began to grow even more restless. For several days the pack closed in tight again, and they could no longer detect the movement of the ocean. But they knew it was out there, not far. The weather was growing fouler every day as the Antarctic winter approached, with hard frosts and cold rain. Ice began to build up under the sledge runners beneath the boats, and the crew had to shift the boats from one site to another to keep them from freezing in place: they had to be ready to launch at any moment. Every morning they lashed up and stowed their gear.

But the ice around them still didn't open. On March 23, they spied land to the west, probably one of the Danger Islands at the entrance to Erebus and Terror Gulf—a scant fifty-seven miles away. "If the ice opens we could land in a day," Hurley lamented in his diary. Yet the ice pack, with Patience Camp and its twenty-eight frustrated and helpless men, drifted past.

The men busied themselves with repairs to clothing and equipment, readying themselves for the next stage of the journey. Now there were always at least two men on watch as the stubborn ice began eroding. A biting southerly gale intensified the cold at the same time that the blubber supply ran alarmingly low. Hot food was limited to once a day; the other meals were cold and comfortless.

Four days after Patience Camp passed the Danger Islands, icebergs began bulldozing through the pack. The bergs, with their deep bottoms caught in opposing currents, crashed in zigzagging paths through the ice as far as the men could see. Horrified, the crew of *Endurance* watched as one large berg began plowing in slow motion toward their position. Huge blocks of ice tumbled out of its path, and large floes were churned into chunks. Some of the men swallowed hard and shook hands with their mates. They all knew that if the berg plowed through their camp, there would be no hope of survival, and trying to get out of its unpredictable path was pointless. Shackleton scratched a match alight with his thumbnail, then lit a cigarette as the rogue iceberg blundered toward them.

The men watched it come closer and closer, breathing a sigh of relief when it veered away and passed them to the east. They were spared—for now.

As March continued, the weather turned to rain and then to snow, and the men crawled into their damp sleeping bags in complete, wretched misery. They were hungry, cold, and frightened. Fights broke out for the flimsiest reasons. Some men cried, their tears freezing on their bearded cheeks. The ice men began to believe that they would never be released from their prison. Shackleton did what he could to encourage his men, going from one tent to the next and asking how they were, or starting conversations on topics totally unrelated to their present dangers.

Then, during the early morning hours of March 28, their floe split in half. "Crack!" came a yell from Cheetham, on watch. "Lash up and stow!" As the men struggled out of their tents, they saw two cracks running through their floe; the edges rose and fell in a strong swell. Each man knew his emergency orders. Some dashed to the boats and began heaving and cracking them out of the night's ice; others broke down the camp and began stowing tents and gear. Macklin rounded up his team of dogs—the last of the dogs—and got them in order. Some of the men saw with alarm that their seal meat supply was on a piece of floe that was beginning to drift away in the heavy mist, so they jumped the widening crack and began tossing the meat over. Once all the men and gear were safe on the same piece of floe with the boats, they began to relax, only to have another crack split directly under the *James Caird*. Another scramble in the chilly, damp morning followed. Finally, they dared to eat a cold breakfast.

Just as they were finishing, a leopard seal loomed through the mist, hunching itself across the ice. Wild ran for his rifle and brought the seal down with one bullet, and when the eleven-foot-long animal was butchered, the men discovered fifty undigested fish inside its stomach. Minutes earlier, the crew had been on short rations eaten cold. Now they had 1,000 pounds of meat and at least two weeks' worth of blubber. Shackleton announced they would make a holiday feast on the seal's liver at lunchtime.

And yet, in spite of the new bounty of food, it was time for the last dogs to go. It was obvious to everyone that the pack was breaking up all around them, and it would be impossible to take the dogs in the boats. Macklin harnessed his team for the last time and drove them some distance from the camp with Wild. Sick with regret, Macklin took his dogs one by one from harness. Wild took each unsuspecting animal behind a hummock of ice and quickly put a bullet in its brain. Then

Macklin skinned and butchered the dogs for meat and brought them back to camp. Later, as the men feasted on the dogs, Worsley commented that the piece he was eating had a better flavor than the leopard seal, and Hurley found it "exquisitely tender and flavorous." As Hurley later wrote, "A casual observer might think the Explorer a frozen-hearted individual, especially if he noticed the mouths watering when tears ought to be expected. Hunger brings us all to the level of other species, and our saying that 'sledge dogs are born for work & bred for food' is but the rationale of experience."

Overhead, terns and Cape pigeons wheeled, and a giant snow petrel flew on snow-white wings; the birds were a sure sign that open water was near. In an open lead of water, Clark spotted some jellyfish, another sign of open ocean. They were very close.

Shackleton now ordered the men to keep "watch and watch," four hours on and four hours off, and to sleep fully dressed in boots, mittens, and hats. The men lay down to sleep on a floe that rose and fell at least a foot with the swell, and some of them felt seasick after so long on a motionless, frozen ocean.

"Our little boats may be compelled any day now to sail unsheltered over the open sea," Shackleton wrote in his diary, "with a thousand leagues of ocean separating them from the land to the north and east. It seems vital that we should land on Clarence Island or its neighbor, Elephant Island." These islands to the northwest were at the very end of the Antarctic Peninsula; beyond them lay the open ocean. If the crew did not reach one of the islands, their chances of survival were very small.

The days continued to wear on, and their floe continued to erode. By April 3, it was only 200 yards across, surrounded by open water and continually bumping into other floes. The sounds of the ice grinding and crushing, creaking and cracking, filled the cold, damp air all around them. All around them, too, were signs that the Antarctic winter was fast approaching: there were now twelve hours of darkness, and during the daylight hours petrels and terns fled toward the north. Skuas kept up a screeching clamor, and penguins on the move honked and brayed from the ice for miles around. Killer whales cruised the open leads, blowing spouts of icy spray. The tricks of the Antarctic atmosphere brought mock suns and green sunsets, and showers of jewel-colored ice crystals.

The floe beneath Patience Camp cracked again and again over the next several days. By April 8, there were open leads of black water on all sides, and the floe was rising and falling three feet with the ocean swell—the ice pack as far as the eye could see was rippling with it, like a box of giant jigsaw puzzle pieces being stirred by a giant hand. The floe was now a mere fifty yards across. The voyagers had traveled 600 miles since *Endurance* was first trapped in the ice.

At twelve forty on April 8, Shackleton gave the order: "Launch the boats."

ESCAPE FROM THE ICE

Thousands of birds accompanied the three boats as the crew got under way. Fulmars, terns, snow petrels, and Cape pigeons filled the sky. The men leaning to the oars were pelted with bird droppings as they tried to accustom themselves to the new circumstances. The sides of all the boats had been raised for protection against rough seas, but that made the seats too low for rowing. The men had to sit awkwardly on crates and packing cases in order to dig their oars into the water at the proper angle. Long out of practice, the rowers fumbled and cursed as they tried to find a rhythm. The wind was bitter, but it was impossible to row fast enough to keep warm—the danger of ramming into the large chunks of brash ice that surrounded them was too great. The swell crashing on the windward side of the great blue tabular icebergs threw spray sixty feet into the air and down onto the boats, where it froze on the men. Those who weren't rowing ducked their heads down against the spray and the bird droppings, and kept a wary eye out for killer whales.

In the lead was the *James Caird,* the largest boat, with Shackleton, Wild, and ten of the men—McIlroy, Wordie, Hussey, James, Clark, Hurley, McCarthy, Green, McNeish, and Vincent. Behind them was the *Dudley Docker,* steered by Worsley and manned by another eight—Greenstreet, Cheetham, Kerr, Macklin, Marston, Orde-Lees, McLeod, and Holness. Bringing up the rear was the *Stancomb Wills,* with Crean and Hudson in command of the remaining five men—Rickinson, How, Bakewell, Stevenson, and Blackborrow, the stowaway, who had good reason to regret his decision to sneak aboard *Endurance.*

The going was slow as they picked a gingerly course through the ice, but they were making progress. Within an hour they had pulled at least a mile away from Patience Camp, which was now lost forever in the broken pack behind them. The men began to think they were truly on their way at last, when a strange rumbling noise reached their ears.

At first they could see nothing, and then from the east-south-east came a thick flow of ice on a riptide current, like a wide river of tumbling, churning chunks and floes. It was barreling straight toward them at a rate of three miles an hour. With a shout to the other boats, Shackleton brought the *Caird* around, and the men began to row as hard as they could. The riptide was roaring after them, threatening to engulf the three puny boats with a deluge of ice and slush. The men who were not rowing stamped their feet in time to help the rowers keep a steady rhythm with the oars. Twice the *Docker* was almost caught, but each time she pulled clear. For fifteen minutes, the three boats fled from the flood of ice, and then just as suddenly as it had appeared, it faded away, and the water grew calm again. The exhausted rowers collapsed over the oars and were pulled aside by the other men, who took their places. Bobbing blue ice and crumbling floes rose and fell with the waves all around them as they brought the boats back onto a course for the northwest.

They continued pulling all afternoon, still dodging through open leads and around large floes and bergs. As the light began to fade, Shackleton began looking out for a good, strong floe to camp on. Eventually one was spotted, and the men were happy to see it was inhabited by a large crabeater seal. By six thirty all hands were pitching tents, and Green was firing up the blubber stove to make dinner out of the seal. By eight o'clock everyone except the watch was fast asleep with the sound of waves slapping and splashing against the edges of their camp.

But then: "An intangible feeling of uneasiness made me leave my tent about 11 P.M.," Shackleton wrote. The heavy swell had changed and was now crashing into their floe head on. "I had started to walk across the floe to warn the watchman to look carefully for cracks when the floe lifted on the crest of a swell and cracked under my feet as I was passing the men's tent. The men were in one of the dome-shaped tents, and it began to stretch apart as the ice opened. . . . I rushed forward, helped some men to come out from under the canvas. . . . The crack had widened to about four feet, and . . . I saw a whitish object floating in the water."

"Somebody's missing!" one of the men yelled as the tent's occupants scrambled to safety in the darkness.

The whitish object in the water was a sleeping bag with Ernest Holness inside it. The Boss leaned over to grab the sodden bag and heaved it—and

Holness—out of the freezing water and onto the ice, just as the two edges of the floe crashed back together.

Then the crack opened once more, separating the camp. Holness's mates began walking him up and down to warm him, because there were no dry clothes into which he could change. Ice crackled off his clothes and fell tinkling onto the floe as the rest of the crew drew the two halves of the floe together again by hauling on a rope. After sledding the *James Caird* across to the larger piece of floe, the men jumped to safety with the rest of the crew. Shackleton remained behind to ensure that all of his men got over safely.

And the floes began to separate again. Shackleton hauled on his end of the rope, but one man's strength was not equal to the force of the ocean pulling the floes apart. As his crew watched in horror, he drifted out of sight into the darkness.

"Launch a boat," he called, just as Wild gave the same order. The *Stancomb Wills* was shoved into the water to rescue him.

As Worsley commented, "The few minutes that it took to fetch Shackleton were among the most anxious I have ever known."

Once the entire crew was reassembled, it was time to turn their attention to Holness, who was in serious danger of freezing to death. Green fired up the blubber stove in order to get some hot milk into the sailor.

"You all right, Holness?" Shackleton asked him.

"Y-yes, B-b-boss," the man chattered, shivering uncontrollably. "Only thing I'm thinking about is my 'baccy [tobacco] I'd left in the bag."

The men dared not return to their tents. Instead, they sought the warmth of the fire for the rest of the night. "Crowded round the little stove with its smoky flickery blubber flames we looked like hobgoblins," Macklin wrote. Every two hours until morning the cook served another round of seal steaks to keep up the men's strength. In the darkness at the edge of the floe, killer whales spouted gustily.

"In spite of our troubles and losing sleep the whole party was in good spirits, for, at last, we had exchanged inaction for action," Worsley remembered. "We had been waiting and drifting at the mercy of the pack ice. There had been nothing that we could do to escape. Now there were more dangers and hardships, but we were working and struggling to save ourselves. We were full of hope and optimism—feelings that Shackleton always fostered."

By 5:00 A.M. the first hint of daylight glowed dimly in the east, and daybreak brought a chilly, misty, overcast day with snow squalls driving in ragged veils across the ice. The men were more than ready to leave the unlucky floe behind, and once the boats were launched, they continued rowing through the pack with a cold easterly wind at their cheeks, trying to make their way north as much as the crowding ice allowed. The weather made it impossible to get a sun sight, but Worsley's best guess put Clarence and Elephant isles about thirty or forty miles north.

Throughout the morning they continued to row toward these small landfalls, and then, at about eleven o'clock, they suddenly broke free of the pack and found themselves in open ocean. Amid much rejoicing, the crews of the three small boats raised sail and forged ahead, spray breaking over their bows and freezing on the men and all the contents of the boats.

The rejoicing was short-lived. "We rounded the north end of the pack," Worsley explained, "but found that in the open the sea was too heavy for our deeply laden boats. Besides the weight of twenty-eight men, we had three tents, spare clothing, our sleeping bags, 'Primus' lamps and paraffin, oars, masts, sails, and three weeks' food for the party. . . .

"We returned to the shelter of the pack, unloaded, and hauled the boats up on a floeberg at 3:30 P.M. There we abandoned one week's supply of food. While we pitched the tents and secured the boats, Green raided the abandoned stores. Presently he produced the best and largest meal we had eaten for five months."

They had finally escaped from the pack, but the open ocean had proved too much for their small fleet. They were back in the ice.

PASSAGE TO ELEPHANT ISLAND

The ocean that had chased them back and made them flee for the shelter of the ice pack is the worst ocean on the globe. The weather systems, with winds of up to 200 miles per hour that howl up from Antarctica, are one reason it is so treacherous. The other reason is geography. Unlike the other continents, Antarctica is completely surrounded by ocean, and there is no significant land to obstruct the rushing waves. Ocean rollers can travel 12,000 miles around the globe at the sixtieth parallel and never bump into anything. The spinning of the earth causes these mighty waves to spiral endlessly to the east, building momentum as they go. They squeeze through Drake's Passage, the gap between the tip of South America and the end of the Antarctic Peninsula, a distance of only 620 miles. This bottleneck compacts the waves and gives them even more force. They can reach 100 feet in height from the bottom of the trough to the crest, and the distance from one wave to the next can measure a mile. They are huge walls of water bearing down on everything in their path at speeds of up to fifty miles an hour. When Sir Francis Drake first navigated through this perilous strait in 1578, it took him sixteen days and cost him four of his ships.

In addition to these waves, known as Cape Horn Rollers, the Southern Ocean carries strange currents that often run against the prevailing winds, causing a broken, turbulent surface and stirring up storms, forcing the waves to mount even higher. Giant "rogue waves" can overtake and reinforce each other, and often come in groups of three. The ancient mariners gave them the superstitious name of "Three Sisters Waves." The tiny outcroppings of rocks and lonesome islets in the extreme south are littered with the wreckage of dead ships. A calm day on the Southern Ocean has swells of fifteen feet.

In the winter the frigid air that flows north from the Pole creates one cyclone after another and collides with warmer air from the tropics, spinning off gales, hurricanes, and blizzards. Spindrift whipping off the crests of breaking waves freezes into sleet. Water is hurled up into the sky and dashed back again. Winds scream over the waves. The sun retreats in horror.

That is the Southern Ocean in winter.

The three boats of the Imperial Trans-Antarctic Expedition ran from the force of the Southern Ocean back into the pack. After scouting around, the men landed the boats on a remnant of a tabular iceberg—a large, flat, blue ice cube that rose about twenty feet from the surface of the water. At the lowest point, the berg was only five feet above the surface. The crew chucked the stores and equipment up, climbed up onto the ice, and hauled the boats after them. Everything in the boats had been soaked with flying spray and breaking waves, but they pitched their camp and crawled into their damp sleeping bags, nursing their blistered and frostbitten hands. They hadn't slept in thirty-six hours.

As they slept, the gale increased, battering other floes against their berg and chipping away at its edges. When they awoke on April 11, their hearts sank. They were caught like rats in a trap. From one horizon to the other, the loose pack had closed in around their camp. Massive thirty-foot ocean rollers from the northwest spooled through the pack, lifting the ice and letting it fall again at half-mile intervals.

"It was as magnificent and beautiful a sight as I have ever seen," Worsley said later. "But it was a sight we did not like, for the floes were thudding against our floeberg with increasing violence. Our temporary home was being swept away at an unpleasantly rapid rate."

The men could only watch helplessly as the mighty waves jostled the ice together. Launching the boats now would be suicidal, but chances were they were about to be pitched into the water at any moment. Huge chunks of ice were breaking away from their berg all the time. Shackleton, Wild, and Worsley kept a lookout from the highest point on their berg, a twenty-foot-tall knoll. All morning they scanned the ocean around them, searching for open water as their floe was whittled down to the size of a tennis court. One lead after another passed them by too far away to reach. But then, two hours after noon, a good open lead reached them, just as their berg began rolling to the side.

"Launch the boats," Shackleton called out. "Chuck in the stores any old way!"

Within minutes they were under way again, dodging their way through the sea of ice. For two hours they made steady progress at the oars, and then Shackleton judged the way clear enough to hoist sail. Immediately, the *James*

Caird sprang ahead, with the *Dudley Docker* nipping along in its wake, but the *Stancomb Wills* fell farther and farther astern. Shackleton, in the *Caird,* grew increasingly anxious as the third boat fell behind. Finally, he drew up in the lee of a large berg and shouted to Worsley to go back and help the other boat. Worsley brought the *Docker* around, and beat back into the wind to take the *Wills* in tow.

Night was falling quickly, but no one wanted to risk another close call like the one they'd had that morning. They sailed into the shelter of a large floe and moored to it. Green climbed up onto the ice and got the stove going to boil up some milk, while several men in the boats mooed like impatient calves. Soon they all held steaming mugs of hot milk, and Green and the blubber stove were brought back on board.

But no sooner had they warmed themselves with the milk then the wind shifted and brought dangerous chunks of ice crowding and bumping up against their floe. The men poled the chunks away with their oars as well as they could, but the danger of being "holed" by ice was too great. With towropes joining the three boats together, they cast off and rowed wearily from one floe to another throughout the night, trying to find some shelter. As the temperature sank below zero, the men took turns at the oars to keep warm. Rain turned to snow showers. It was a very long night.

When the morning came, a northwest breeze brought warmer air, raising the temperature almost up to the freezing point, but with rain and sleet falling, the men were still covered in ice. At noon the sky was clear enough for Worsley to take a sight. Braced against the mast of the *Docker,* he aligned his sextant with the horizon and "shot" the sun. The crew waited anxiously as he worked his calculations. He checked his figures, frowning, and checked them again. He looked up, crestfallen.

"What have we made, Skipper?" Shackleton called from the *James Caird* as he brought the boat alongside the *Docker* and jumped aboard.

Worsley spoke low, so only the Boss could hear. "Thirty miles astern, sir." A current had driven them backward, in spite of all their efforts. They were farther from their destination than when they had launched the boats at Patience Camp.

Shackleton decided not to tell the men how bad it was. "We haven't done as well as we expected," he told the crew.

With dark looks at Worsley, as though they held the navigator responsible, the men brought the boats into the wind again and continued sailing. What else could they do?

That night again they tried to take shelter in the boats in the lee of a large ice floe, but within hours of mooring themselves, the wind changed direction and began battering them against their shelter. The boats cracked loudly against the ice, grating and scraping on the edge of the floe. Shouting over the wind, the men fought their way off and into the open water again, where a heavy, wet snow began falling on them. Around them the sea was stiffening as it froze, and the men could hear the snow crackle as it fell onto the waves. The new sea ice hissed and creaked as it rose on the swell. For the rest of the night, the men sat in the boats, their clothes freezing on them, huddling together for warmth. It was too cold for sleep.

When the light dawned in the morning, they were like a company of ghosts, their faces drained and pale with strain, their beards and hair white with snow and salt spray. Shackleton ordered the sails raised and led the way through the loose pack and pancake ice again. Late in the morning they passed a stretch of ice where thousands of fish had been killed by a cold current. Now fulmars and petrels swooped down and bore them away.

The frigid wind from the Pole increased steadily, driving them northward until, almost without warning, they burst free from the pack and into the open ocean again. Huge ocean rollers swept toward them, and the three boats began clawing up waves whose faces were a quarter of a mile long. The gale force wind tore the crests from the rollers, covering the men and boats with a layer of ice. Before them was the Southern Ocean, and they were making for an island only twenty miles long and 100 miles away. The men prayed that Worsley's calculations were right. They were looking for a needle in a haystack. Beyond Elephant Island lay the 600 miles of Drake's Passage, with no landfall before South America.

Waves broke over the bows of the boats, washing over the exhausted men. Now they had a new agony—a gagging, unbearable thirst. They had left the pack so suddenly that they had not had time to take ice on board for melting into water. Constantly drenched in salt water, the men began to dehydrate. Even without drinking, they had to urinate frequently because of the water absorbed through their skin. They were also tormented by diarrhea from the uncooked meat they had been forced to eat. The only way to relieve themselves was by hanging over the side of the boat as ice seas surged up against them. Shackleton suggested that all hands eat as much as they could in compensation, but few of them could manage to choke down uncooked seal meat or dry sugar cubes, and some were too seasick even to try.

Of the three boats, the *Stancomb Wills* was in the worst fix. It was the small-est, and the least seaworthy. Hudson, who had the tiller, was on the point of breaking. Shackleton and Worsley were terrified that the *Wills* would be lost in the night if they didn't tether it to their boats. As darkness fell on the ocean, the three boats tied themselves together, and the *Docker* put out a sea anchor to keep them turned up into the wind. They had to wait out another night without sleep.

The temperature dropped and the wind kept up, sluicing water over their bows. The men's feet were swamped with cold water. As they began to lose feel-ing, they started wiggling their toes inside their waterlogged boots to keep the blood circulating. With every movement the men made, ice crackled off their clothing. Some of the men began to cry in their despair; some shouted curses to the wind through cracked and frostbitten lips. The fear of killer whales tangling in their lines began to prey on some of the men's minds, and all of them could feel the motion of the boats growing clumsier and heavier as ice built up on them. They were shipping water constantly. The men took turns hacking ice off the thwarts and bows, and bailing to keep the small boats from foundering.

Gradually, in the small hours of the morning, the wind stopped flaying them and began to taper off. When the sun finally rose in a brilliant pink sky, it shone on twenty-eight men who were more dead than alive. Saltwater boils on their faces were breaking open and dripping across the dead-white rings of frostbite. Their eyes were sunken and red, and they had the wild look of men driven to the end of their ropes by pain and exposure. But dead ahead, not more than thirty miles away, rose the snow-covered basalt peaks of Elephant Island. Some of the men laughed, nearly hysterical. In a cracked voice, the Boss ordered the sea anchor brought in. By the impossibly beautiful light of the sunrise, he looked like an old man. Worsley noted it with shock. Somehow, Shackleton had always seemed invincible, but even the Boss had been beaten hard by the terrible night.

With luck, however, they would be on land by the next nightfall. A steady breeze filled their sails, but to the men, it didn't drive them fast enough. They shoved their oars into the water again and, with land in sight, found strength they didn't know they had. Some of them chewed raw seal meat to swallow the blood and ease their parched throats. Most of them had not slept in more than three days, but they could see the end of their ordeal over the breaking waves. The *James Caird* still towed the clumsy *Wills* for safety, and the *Docker* dragged itself forward in the lead.

Blackborrow had lost all feeling in his feet. There was almost nothing anyone could do for him, but Dr. McIlroy massaged the young man's feet, trying to restore the circulation. Greenstreet and Macklin also took off their boots and found their feet frostbitten, but they rubbed their toes until they felt the searing pain of blood flowing through their veins.

Steadily, throughout the day, the three boats drew nearer and nearer to Elephant Island. By two in the afternoon they were less than ten miles away. But at three o'clock they hadn't gotten any closer. They were in the grip of a current that held them off the island. To make matters worse, the wind shifted around and began holding them off as well. The sails were lowered hastily, and the men redoubled their efforts at the oars. It was too cruel to believe, but they could not get closer to the island.

As darkness began to fall at five thirty, the wind shifted once again and quickly blew up into a gale, tearing the tops off the waves. Worsley shouted to Shackleton that their best hope now lay in separating; he was having trouble keeping the nimble *Dudley Docker* back with the other two boats. Reluctantly, Shackleton agreed, although he refused to release the tether that kept the *Wills* with the *Caird*. He was sure that if he let the smaller boat go, it would never be seen again. The wind ripped clouds across the face of the moon. By the faint light, Worsley steered the *Docker* toward Elephant Island and was soon lost to sight.

It was night, and they were still in the boats. The men were sick with disappointment. Some of them lay senseless and numb, on the brink of losing their minds. Shackleton feared that some of the men would die if they didn't make landfall soon. Once during the night he called out in the darkness to the *Wills*.

"Blackborrow!"

"Here, sir," came a weak reply.

"We shall be on Elephant Island tomorrow," the Boss shouted. "No one has ever landed there before, and you will be the first ashore."

Blackborrow did not answer. He had long since lost all feeling in his feet, and doubted he would land anywhere, first or last.

On the *Docker*, the men were clawing their way toward the island in heavy seas. The boat pitched and rolled wildly as waves smashed into it broadside. Worsley had only one compass left, and he lighted a match to check that they were still headed in the right direction: the island itself was lost in the darkness. Cheetham had been smoking, but his pipe had gone out, and he begged a match from Worsley to relight it. The other men let out a storm of protest at using up their precious matches.

"Look here, I'll sell you one," Worsley said.

"Right, sir. What price?" the third officer asked.

With a hoarse laugh, Worsley replied, "A bottle of champagne."

"Done, sir. As soon as I get back to Hull and open my little pub, the champagne's yours."

They sat through the rest of the night, bailing, rowing, and cursing. Worsley, who had been at the tiller for more than fifty hours, finally pitched forward in a dead faint. Greenstreet took the tiller and prayed he would stay on the right course. When the morning dawned, foggy and squally, they were right up under the island's towering black cliffs, and a violent squall tore down the side of a mountain, slamming into the boat.

"Wake Worsley!" Greenstreet cried.

The men tried to rouse the skipper, calling and shaking him, but he seemed to be dead. McLeod gave Worsley a couple of hard kicks to the head. Instantly, Worsley sat up and croaked, "Keep her away four points." Waves thundered against the rocks, throwing spray into the air and falling back with a hiss.

Worsley steered the boat westward, searching for a landing site. Dominican gulls sailed up the black peaks, disappearing into the fog. By nine thirty the crew of the *Docker* still hadn't found a beach, and there was no sight of the other two boats.

"Poor blighters," Greenstreet whispered, sure the *Caird* and the *Wills* were lost at sea. "They're gone."

Then they rounded a spit, and ahead of them were the other boats, standing off in the surf where a reef sent breakers crashing up into the air. A narrow tongue of land made a landing beach at the base of the cliffs. The feeble shouts of the men on the *Docker* were lost in the pounding of the waves. Shackleton waited for an opening in the surf and then gave a shout for the men to pull with their last strength through the reef. Shingle scraped beneath the bow as the boat ground up onto the shore.

"Jump ashore, Blackborrow," Shackleton urged, determined to give his youngest crewman the honor of first landing.

Blackborrow didn't move. Impatient, Shackleton reached out and dragged the boy up by his arms and hoisted him over the side. Blackborrow fell to his hands and knees, and a breaking wave toppled him over.

"Get up," Shackleton ordered.

"I can't, sir," the boy replied.

In a flood of shame, Shackleton remembered that Blackborrow's feet were frozen. He motioned How and Bakewell over the side to help the young man onto shore. One by one the boats surged up onto the rocky beach, and the crew stumbled through the water, on solid ground for the first time in sixteen months. Wild stepped out of the *Caird* beside Shackleton "as easy and unconcerned as if he had stepped out of his car for a stroll in the park," the Boss recalled later. But most of the men were not as calm as Wild. Many of them began weeping and laughing at the same time, falling to their hands and knees to pick up black pebbles and let them trickle through their hands.

They had landed.

DRY LAND

Elephant Island had been named years earlier for the throngs of elephant seals that crowded its rocky shores. Seals and birds were its only residents. Only twenty miles long and thirteen miles wide, it lies at the farthest tip of the Antarctic Peninsula. Beyond it stretches Drake's Passage. By navigating there through fog, snow, and winter seas, Worsley had found the needle in the haystack.

True to its name, the island presented them with an elephant seal on landing. Almost immediately, the animal was converted into food. Green began cooking again, although without his usual smile. For the first several hours on land, the men ate, slept, and ate again, standing around in small groups, stupefied and silent. From a penguin colony nearby, gentoos waddled down the beach to stare at their visitors.

Shackleton and Worsley walked some distance along the beach, sizing up their location. It was a desolate spot. "Thank God I haven't killed one of my men," the Boss said. "I knew that one more night of exposure would do for some of them." They walked in silence for a few moments, their feet crunching in the loose rocks, and then Shackleton added, "What do you think of this place, Skipper?"

"Any solid land is a godsend when we are so badly in need of rest and food," Worsley admitted. "But I've looked round a bit and—well, it's not much like the Riviera."

It was quite an understatement. Grim black cliffs reached up 800 feet into the fog at their backs, and the 2,500-foot peaks behind those were covered with glaciers and snow. Cormorants, skuas, and Cape pigeons wheeled in and out of the mist. Patches of orange lichen made the only bright color, and a high-water mark on the cliff walls showed that their landing site was not at all safe. Storm tides would frequently submerge their spit of land when the weather turned ugly. They would have to find a better beach before deciding what to do next.

But before anything could be done, the men needed to rest. Through the remainder of the day and night, they slept and ate, keeping the fire going in the stove with the blubber from four more seals they slaughtered on the beach. Shackleton let the crew sleep until nine thirty the next morning. Then he told them the news. They would soon have get back in the boats and move.

At eleven, Frank Wild and five men pushed the *Wills* out into the crashing surf and rowed off in search of a new landing site. A couple of miles offshore, a belt of pack ice and eroded bergs was drifting past, warning everyone of the winter to come. Meanwhile, the men continued to eat and rest, enjoying the feel of solid ground under their feet, stretching their cramped limbs, melting glacier ice into drinking water. They moved the stores and tents as high up the spit as possible and waited for Wild's party to return.

Darkness had fallen by the time the *Wills* ground onto the shingle beach again. Tired and hungry, Wild devoured a seal steak as he described their nine hours of searching the coastline. The only suitable place they had found was seven miles to the west. It was another narrow spit of land, with a penguin rookery and a glacier nosing down the mountainside nearby. The Boss decided they should set out at dawn.

At five o'clock the next morning, with the stores loaded onto the boats, the men pushed off into the water again, rowing along the base of the cliffs. Within two hours the winds picked up, quickly blowing into hurricane force, crashing waves against the rocks and hurling spray over the men in the boats, where it froze into slush. They struggled forward against a hard current, sometimes seeming to stand still despite their straining at the oars. The boats rolled and pitched in the violent, sucking backwash from the cliffs. Somehow, Greenstreet had lost his mittens, and the blisters on his hands froze like pebbles under the skin. Macklin, too, lost a mitten, and his hand turned white with frostbite on his oar. For hours they battled their way westward in a blizzard. By three o'clock the beach was in sight, and with a last effort they dragged themselves through the breakers and hauled the boats out of reach of the waves. Some of the men immediately killed a seal that was resting on the rocks, and Greenstreet staggered toward it and thrust his frozen hands into the bloody, steaming carcass.

The beaten men stumbled on numb feet to examine their new campsite. It was only a faint improvement over the first one, bare and exposed to the wind. Sharp, sudden gusts carried away some of their stores the moment they were set down and ripped one of the threadbare tents to shreds. But the beach rose steep above the high-tide mark. At least they would not be swept away in a storm.

It was impossible to set up the tents with the wind shrieking around them. The men slept exposed on the ground, with snow drifting up against their backs. The blizzard continued for two days, and no one dared crawl from the protection of his sleeping bag or blanket. On April 17, after two days at the new site, Shackleton ordered the men out to kill penguins. They skinned the birds with frozen hands, choking on wind-driven snow with each breath.

Shackleton knew—everyone knew—that they could not hold out on that desolate spot all winter. The seals and penguins might not last, and even if they made it to summer, whaling ships rarely came anywhere near Elephant Island: no one knew to look for them there. Someone would have to go for help. The closest inhabited land was Cape Horn, at the tip of South America, 600 miles away. But sailing due north across Drake's Passage in the winter would be suicide. All the winds and waves would be against it. The only possible course was to take advantage of the prevailing winds and currents and make for South Georgia Island, 800 miles to the east. Worsley and Shackleton had known for months that it was their only hope.

"Skipper, we shall have to make that boat journey, however risky it is," the Boss said. "I'm not going to let the men starve."

Worsley's voice was almost swallowed by the wind. "Would you let me take the boat?" he asked, believing the leader should stay with the men.

"No," Shackleton replied sharply. "That's my job." He paused, glancing back at his crew. "It's hateful to have to tell the men that we've got to leave them."

"It's their only chance," Worsley said.

Shackleton looked very grim. "If things went wrong, it might be said that I had abandoned them."

His responsibility had never been greater. Shackleton consulted with Wild, who demanded a place on the boat beside his leader, but Shackleton was relying on his second-in-command to hold the men together while they waited for rescue. Then he gathered the men to break the news. He would take the *James Caird* and go for help.

Immediately, every man stepped forward to volunteer. Choosing a crew was difficult. Worsley must go along: no one else was capable of the navigating that this journey would require, and his experience with small boats was unmatched. Crean, the seasoned explorer, was fit to go. Shackleton also chose Tim McCarthy, one of the seamen who had remained cheerful and steadfast through all their troubles, and who was young and strong. In spite of Shackleton's enduring resentment of McNeish ever since his mutiny, he resolved that the carpenter must go, in order to make running repairs to the boat. Last, Shackleton chose John Vincent, another of the seamen who was young and strong—and also something of a troublemaker. Shackleton chose Vincent to keep him away from the other men. They would leave in four days.

Meanwhile, there was much to get ready. McNeish began refitting the twenty-two-foot-long *Caird* for the journey, decking it over with packing crate lids and canvas, and raising the sides. The keel was reinforced with the *Docker*'s mast. Canvas bags were stitched together from sails and filled with 1,000 pounds of rocks for ballast, and two kegs were filled with glacier melt for drinking water. The boat's stores would include one of the Primus camp stoves, six weeks' worth (for six men) of sledging rations for "hoosh," and some bouillon cubes, sugar, powdered milk, and biscuits. Worsley's navigational equipment was down to one compass, his sextant, and his tables—and of the twenty-four chronometers he had taken with him from London, he had only one remaining. The job ahead of him was formidable.

On the night before departure, the men were anxious and restless. Wild and Greenstreet joked with Worsley, telling him to be sure to bring back plenty of beer. Shackleton shared his last two cigarettes with Wild as they discussed backup plans. The Boss wrote and signed a letter with his instructions: if he did not return with a relief ship, Wild was to take the men in the remaining two boats and try to save themselves.

The six-man relief team was ready to set out the next morning.

DRY LAND

93

THE OPEN BOAT JOURNEY: THE FIRST TEN DAYS

On the morning of Monday, April 24, all hands were roused at six o'clock to help lash up and stow the *Caird*. As Wild oversaw the preparation of the boat, Shackleton and Worsley climbed up a small hill they used as a lookout and surveyed the ocean. The ice was within five or six miles of the shore, drifting northeast. Large, grounded icebergs made wide gaps in the ice as they streamed past them. The rescue party would escape through one of those leads.

Below, the *Caird* was dragged down to the surf and loaded with the bags of ballast, boxes of stores, a hand pump, a cook pot, six reindeer-skin sleeping bags, and the rest of the provisions. At noon the men heaved the laden boat out on the backwash of a breaking wave, and the remainder of the stores was ferried out on the *Stancomb Wills*. Shackleton and Worsley rejoined the group. There were handshakes all around. The six members of the relief party boarded the boat, and they shoved off.

Behind on the beach, the remaining twenty-two men cheered and waved. "Good luck, Boss!" they shouted. Shackleton looked back once and raised his hand in farewell. Gentoo penguins porpoised along beside the boat as they raised the sail and plunged forward into the rolling waves. The Boss stood with one arm around the mast looking forward, directing Worsley at the helm around the ice.

They made good speed for two hours and then reached the loose belt of ice they had seen from the lookout. They turned east along it, searching for the leads that would let them through. Huge, lopsided remnant bergs bobbed and heaved in the waves, and small chunks of broken floe knocked and scraped along the sides of the *Caird*. The whole jumble of loose pack hissed and rustled as it rose to the swell. After an hour's run, they found an opening and turned north to sail through it. Just before dark they were on the other side, and when they looked over their shoulders they saw Elephant Island as a small shadow far astern.

Shackleton and Worsley had agreed that the safest plan was to get as far north as possible before heading east. For one thing, they would be glad to get away from the most frigid weather as soon as they could. Furthermore, they would be sailing day and night, and they needed to get beyond the limit of floating ice: if they rammed a chunk in the dark, their journey would be a short one. By 10:00 P.M. the water seemed relatively clear of ice, and their spirits rose: so far, so good. In the darkness, they steered by keeping an eye on the small blue pennant that streamed from the mast in the wind.

The living arrangements on board were uncomfortable and cramped. The men were divided into two watches: Shackleton, Crean, and McNeish steered, bailed, and pumped for four hours, while Worsley, Vincent, and McCarthy slept—or tried to. Then the watches traded places—watch and watch, every four hours. The sleeping bags were forward, under the improvised decking on the bow. To reach them, the men had to crawl on hands and knees over the stone ballast, then wriggle forward on their stomachs over the crates of stores. Then, with barely enough room to turn around, they wormed themselves into the sleeping bags and attempted to sleep as the boat bucked up and down through the heavy swell. At the end of each four-hour watch, the men would change places, wriggling past each other in the cramped space.

It was a tossup which was worse—being pounded up and down in the bow of the boat in a sorry excuse for sleep, or huddling in the cockpit as icy seas swept across the thwarts and gunwales. There were no oilskins, and the men were dressed in wool, which got wet and stayed wet for the duration of the voyage. With temperatures below freezing, and no room to move around to get their blood stirred up, they were always cold. Miserably cold. Waves broke over the bows, where bucketfuls of water streamed through the flimsy decking. The bottom of the boat was constantly awash, and the two men on watch who weren't steering were always bailing or pumping. The reindeer-skin sleeping bags were soaking wet all the time, and beginning to rot. Loose reindeer hair found its way into the men's nostrils and mouths as they breathed, into their water and their food as they ate.

Crean had taken over as cook for the journey. In the pitching and rolling of the boat, preparing meals was a tricky business. Crean and Worsley would sit on opposite sides of the boat with their feet out, bracing the Primus camp stove. Crean would light the stove and begin stirring up chunks of sledging

The *James Caird* is launched for the rescue journey to South Georgia Island, April 24, 1916.

ration in water as Worsley held the pot. With each dip and plunge of the boat, Worsley swooped the pot up in the air lest their precious hoosh go slopping into the bilges. When the hoosh was cooked, Crean doled it out into six bowls, and the men ate it scalding hot, hunched under the decking. Whoever finished first went out to relieve the man at the tiller so that he could eat his hoosh before it cooled. In addition, Shackleton allowed hot milk and sugar at regular intervals: the only way to keep going was by fueling themselves constantly.

By the third day of sailing, the weather turned rotten. A gale blew up with snow squalls and heavy seas, and waves broke incessantly over the boat. The *James Caird* clawed its way up the face of one hissing wave and then plunged down the other side as spray lashed into the men's faces. The gale continued into the fourth day, finally blowing them north of the sixtieth parallel. Floating past them went two pieces of wreckage from a lost ship. The men watched it disappear, and hunched their shoulders and struggled to keep their little boat on course. As Shackleton put it, "So small was our boat and so great were the seas that often our sail flapped idly in the calm between the crests of two waves. Then we would climb the next slope, and catch the full fury of the gale where the wool-like whiteness of the breaking water surged around us."

For Worsley, navigating had ceased to be a science and had turned into a kind of sorcery. To get a sight of the sun meant Worsley had to kneel on the thwart, where Vincent and McCarthy would hug him around the waist to keep him from pitching out of the boat as it bucked and leaped over the waves. Then, while Shackleton stood by with the chronometer, Worsley would wait until the boat reached the top of the wave and the horizon came into sight, then shout "Now!" as he shot the sun. His books were fast turning into useless pulp. His sun sights were the crudest of guesses, and to look up positions in the tables he had to peel apart the wet pages one by one. Making his calculations with a pencil became laughably impossible. The boat pitched and rolled so badly that he could barely read his own scribbles. The weather was so foul that in the whole journey he managed to take a sight of the sun only four times.

Since leaving Elephant Island, the six men had been accompanied by an albatross, who soared and dipped through the air. The bird could have reached South Georgia in a matter of hours, if it chose, while the men in the *James*

Caird were crawling like a beetle over the surface of the ocean. Each time Worsley calculated the number of miles they had put behind them, the bird seemed to mock their slow progress.

On their seventh day at sea, the wind again turned into a gale roaring up from the Pole; the temperature plummeted. The men began to fear that the sails would freeze up and cake with ice, becoming heavier and heavier until the the boat toppled upside down. With the gale howling around their ears, they took down the sails and rolled them up, stuffing them into the cramped space below. Then they rigged a sea anchor, a canvas cone dragged through the water to keep the boat turned into the storm.

Throughout the night, waves crashed over the *James Caird* and quickly turned to ice. At first the crew was relieved, since it meant the flimsy decking was sealed against further leaks. But when they awoke on the eighth day, they felt the clumsy, heavy motion of the boat beneath them and knew they were in trouble: fifteen inches of ice encased the boat above the waterline, and she was rolling badly. "We saw and felt that the *James Caird* had lost her resiliency," Shackleton said later. "She was not rising to the oncoming seas. The weight of the ice was having its effect, and she was becoming more like a log than a boat."

The ice had to come off. Taking turns, the men crawled on hands and knees over the iced deck, hacking away with an ax. "First you chopped a hand-hold, then a kneehold, and then chopped off ice hastily but carefully, with an occasional sea washing over you," Worsley explained. Each man could stand only five minutes or so of this cold and perilous job at a time. Then it was the next man's turn.

And the gale continued through the next day, too. As Shackleton crawled out to relieve Worsley at the tiller, a large wave slammed the skipper right in the face. Shackleton took the tiller ropes and commented, "Pretty juicy," and both men managed a weak laugh.

As the storm continued, a large buildup of ice on the sea anchor's rope had kept the line swinging and sawing against the stern. Before noon on the ninth day, the sea anchor broke away, and the boat lurched heavily as seas hit her broadside. Before the gale ended that afternoon, the men had had to crawl onto the deck three times to get rid of the boat's shell of ice. The men all agreed that it was the worst job any of them had ever been forced to do.

By the time the gale ended, everything below was thoroughly soaked. The sleeping bags were so slimy and revolting that Shackleton had the two worst of them thrown overboard. Even before the storm, however, the men had been suffering from the constant wet. "After the third day our feet and legs had swelled," Worsley wrote later, "and began to be superficially frostbitten from the constant soaking in seawater, with the temperature at times nearly down to zero; and the lack of exercise. During the last gale they assumed a dead-white color and lost surface feeling."

Exposure was beginning to wear the men down. In spite of two hot meals a day, they were hungry for fresh meat. Cape pigeons often darted and flitted around the boat, but the men couldn't bring themselves to kill the friendly birds, and ancient superstition forbade them from killing the albatross that still followed majestically above. But the men were in pain. They were cold, frostbitten, and covered with salt-water blisters. Their legs were rubbed raw from the chafing of their wet pants. Conditions below were almost unbearable: the stinking, rotting sleeping bags made the air putrid, and the molting hairs choked the men as they tried to gasp for breath. Their bodies were bruised and aching from their pounding up and down in the bows, and they were exhausted from lack of sleep. McNeish, who was more than fifty, was beginning to break down. Vincent, who should have stood the conditions well, was also close to collapsing. Shackleton, Worsley, Crean, and McCarthy took up the slack. When someone looked particularly bad, the Boss ordered a round of hot milk for all hands. The one man he really wanted to get the hot drink into never realized that the break was for his benefit and so wasn't embarrassed, and all of the men were better off for having the warmth and nourishment.

The night after the gale ended, Shackleton was at the tiller, crouched in a half-standing, half-sitting position against the thwart with his back hunched against the cold. He glanced back toward the south and saw a line of white along the horizon. "It's clearing, boys!" he shouted. But when he looked back again, he yelled, "For God's sake, hold on! It's got us!" Instead of a clearing sky, the white line to the south was the foaming crest of an enormous storm wave bearing down on them. Worsley was just crawling out of his sleeping bag when the wave struck, and for a few moments the entire boat seemed to be submerged.

Worsley, Crean, Vincent, McCarthy, and McNeish frantically pumped and bailed with anything they could find—the cook pot, dippers, their hands—anything that would get the water out of the boat. For an hour they labored to keep the water from capsizing the *Caird*. They could hardly believe they had not foundered, and they prayed they would not see another wave like that one again.

On the tenth day, the sun showed its face long enough for Worsley to get a fix. He calculated that they had made 444 miles from Elephant Island, more than half the distance. The men rejoiced as the weather cleared and they had the first good weather of the passage. They brought wet sleeping bags and clothes up on deck and hung them from the masts, halyards, and rigging. The sleeping bags and clothing didn't dry, but they were reduced from soaking wet to merely damp. All their spirits were lifted. They were more than halfway to South Georgia Island.

"We were a tiny speck in the vast vista of the sea," Shackleton wrote later. "For a moment the consciousness of the forces arrayed against us would be overwhelming. Then hope and confidence would rise again as our boat rose to a wave and tossed aside the crest in a sparkling shower like the play of prismatic colors at the foot of a waterfall."

They had less than half the distance left to go.

THE END OF THE OPEN BOAT JOURNEY

For three days they had fair weather, although they only had blue skies once when Worsley could manage a sight. They continued bearing eastward, still shipping seas over their bows, still wet and cold. But at least they were not tormented by storms and freak monster waves.

On the twelfth day out from Elephant Island, however, they discovered a potential disaster. When the two casks of fresh water had been brought onto the *James Caird*, one had fallen into the surf and banged against a rock. Now they found that salt water had gotten into it. Shackleton reduced the water ration to half a cup a day. The water had to be strained through gauze to remove the reindeer hair that had gotten into it—the hair had gotten into everything. With red eyes inflamed by wind and salt spray, they stared ahead into the ocean, anxious for a sight of land, licking their cracked lips.

Just before dark on the fourteenth day, they saw a piece of floating kelp. "We joyfully hailed it as a sign of nearness to the land," Worsley wrote. If his calculations were correct, they were only eighty miles from South Georgia Island.

The whaling stations on the island were all on the northeast coast. The *James Caird* would be approaching from the southwest. Shackleton and Worsley debated where they should try to make a landfall. The southwest coastline was mostly uncharted, and they had no idea what kind of coves or natural harbors they could expect. On the other hand, trying to sail around to the other side put them at risk of being swept past the island and into the Atlantic with no landfall before Africa.

"Can you be positive of your position?" the Boss asked Worsley.

"Not to ten miles, but I can easily allow for that," the skipper replied.

Frowning, Shackleton studied the featureless sea ahead of them. They would have to make for the nearer coast, the uninhabited shore. It was the only safe choice.

May 8 was their fifteenth day out from Elephant Island. The day was foggy, and a heavy, cross sea and lumpy waves kept the men miserably wet.

Through the mist they spotted a cormorant, and the men swore those birds never went farther than fifteen miles from land. They were close.

At noon the fog lifted into low clouds that scudded across their bows from the west-northwest. Rain squalls pelted them, hissing into the waves. Then McCarthy cried out, "Land ho!"

Ten miles ahead of them was a towering black mountain spotted with snow. The flying clouds hid it from their sight the next moment, but the men were grinning widely. "We've done it," Shackleton said in a hoarse, cracking voice.

They sailed ahead and by three o'clock could make out the faint patches of green tussock grass that grew among the snowy rocks. But as the sun began to go down in a red, stormy-looking glare, they still had not found a harbor. Swallowing their disappointment, they bore away from the dangerous coast to wait out the night.

"The heavy westerly swell increased," Worsley wrote. "All night the *Caird* fell about in a very dangerous, lumpy, and confused sea, that seemd to run in on us from all directions, so that we sometimes shipped two seas over from opposite sides at the same time."

By dawn it was obvious that the men were in for another storm, and by noon the gale had blown up into hurricane force, lashing them with snow, rain, hail, and sleet. The howling winds were driving them straight toward the rocky coast. With each wave the boat was lifted high into the frenzy of the hurricane and then dropped into the trough, where it was almost becalmed. Each wave thrust them closer to the rocks.

Their only hope lay in trying to sail out of reach. Worsley knew that the boat was so low in the water that the wind had no purchase on the sides of the craft. If they set their two smallest sails, they could crawl up into the wind, away from the shore. It took more than an hour to rig the sails in the racing wind as they clung to the decks. Then the boat began clawing offshore, directly into the onrushing waves. Each sea now smashed with full force into the *Caird*. "While all bailed and pumped for dear life, she seemed to stop, then again charged a galloping wall of water, slam! like striking a stone wall with such force that the bow planks opened and lines of water spurted in from every seam, as she halted, trembling, and then leaped forward again," Worsley wrote.

All afternoon and into the night, the punishment continued. Of all the dangers the men had confronted so far, this seemed to be the worst. They tried not to look back over their shoulders. The crashing of waves behind them told them how close they were to being smashed against the rocks. Shortly after nine that night the hurricane began to decrease. They had fought against it for nine hours. Much later they discovered that the hurricane had foundered a 500-ton steamer from Buenos Aires, sending it to the bottom with all hands.

With the storm over, the first watch crawled into the bows to try to catch some sleep. A meal was out of the question: the water was gone, and their mouths and tongues were so swollen with thirst that they could hardly swallow. When the sun rose, the men stared bleary-eyed at the coast of South Georgia. They had to land that day. Shackleton thought McNeish would probably die if they didn't.

As Crean crawled out of his sleeping bag and began wriggling out from under the decking, his shoulder knocked against a pin that held the mast clamp in place. During the hurricane it had worked itself out until it held only by the tip. Now it fell out, opening the clamp and letting the mast topple forward. McCarthy caught it just in time. Crean held up the fallen pin in wonderment.

"Think of the strain it had been standing all the time, and holding on to the last, as if it knew what it meant to us," Shackleton remarked later. If the mast had fallen during the hurricane, they would have been lost.

Now King Haakon Bay was nine miles ahead of them. Worsley, Vincent, Crean, and McCarthy took turns at their two oars, pulling the boat forward and trying to get into the long fjord. It took all day, tacking against the wind, resetting the sails, rowing, tacking again, and rowing some more. The men scanned the water ahead desperately for floating ice to melt and drink, but found none. The early winter evening was falling when they saw a cove that might give them a good landing.

They pulled in to the entrance with the wind beating against their backs. Waves broke on boulders, sending white spray up into the twilight. Cliffs rose eighty feet high on either side of the cove, but at the southwest corner they spied a rocky beach where they could haul out. Shackleton stood in the bow directing the steering. The oarsmen felt ropes of kelp fouling their strokes with each pull. It was dark when their keel finally scraped over the rocks. They were back on South Georgia after eighteen months. At their feet, pools and streams of glacier melt came running forward to meet the ocean. The men fell on their hands and knees, lapping up the sweet water like dogs.

THE CAVE

Before they could rest, Shackleton ordered the boat unloaded and beached. The men were so tired, and their legs so swollen and painful, that it took hours of staggering up and down the rough beach, into the water and out again. By the time they were finished, they had no strength left to drag the boat up over the rocks, and since there was nothing to tie it to, the men had to take turns through the night holding on to the *James Caird*'s painter as the boat knocked and bumped around the boulders in the breaking surf.

Meanwhile, Crean went exploring and reported a cave not far away. It wasn't exactly a spacious cavern, more an undercut in the face of the cliff, with a curtain of enormous icicles screening the entrance. The six men spread their remaining sodden sleeping bags on the pebbles and fell down, huddling against one another for warmth.

Over the next two days, the men concentrated on getting well. By this time, Vincent and McNeish were complete invalids and stayed in the cave in a stupor. The others—Shackleton, Worsley, Crean, and McCarthy—scouted around their campsite. They found coarse grass to cover and cushion the cave floor. At one end of the cove, an enormous pileup of wreckage from years of storms provided a steady supply of firewood: block and tackle, hatch gratings, spars, masts, lockers. It was a true ships' graveyard. At the end of the long fjord their cove was on, icebergs calved off the ends of twelve or more glaciers with a roar throughout the days that sent birds screeching up into the air.

As the men's feet dried and the blood began to circulate, they all had the sensation of burning. One night, sleeping with his feet near the fire, Worsley woke up repeatedly, sure that his feet *were* actually on fire. The others insisted they all felt the same, and that his feet were fine. It wasn't until the next morning that Worsley discovered holes scorched in his socks, but the skin on his feet was still so waterlogged that it hadn't burned. Their hands and faces were all caked with blubber smoke, soot from the Primus camp stove, and dirt, and some of the men tried washing up in the snow. "The dirt came off in rolls," Worsley said of his hands. But when he applied the same process to his face, he succeeded only in smearing his entire countenance with a more even layer of shiny black grease.

Stumbling on painful feet, they explored the cliff faces nearby. They found albatross chicks, which made the most succulent stews in their hoosh pot. An elephant seal or two increased their food supply. The men ate and slept. In the night once, Shackleton woke them all by shouting in his sleep, "Look out, boys! Look out! Hold on!"

"What is it, Boss?" Worsley asked him.

Fuddled with sleep, Shackleton pointed at the black wall behind them. "It's just going to break on us," he warned, still caught in a dream of monster waves.

After several days of rest, however, it was time for action. They could not linger in their cave all winter, dining on seal meat and toasting their feet at a driftwood fire. The men on Elephant Island were still counting on them. If they took to the sea again, they faced another perilous journey 130 miles around the tip of South Georgia to the whaling stations. And there were serious doubts that the *Caird* could manage another journey at all: the pounding it had taken at sea, and the scraping and bumping it suffered on the beach where they were, had taken their toll on the boat. It was a mere shell, its hull scraped to the thickness of cardboard in some places.

No, the men could not do 130 miles in the *Caird*. But as the crow flies— that was only twenty-nine miles across the island. Shackleton and Worsley eyed the razorback ridges and glaciers that rose up into the clouds. No one had ever crossed South Georgia Island on foot. The Alps of the Southern Ocean were just as formidable as any mountain range, and they were unmapped. But for Shackleton it was the only choice. He was tormented with the thought of the twenty-two men waiting for him. They were waiting for *him*. The Boss. For months they had placed all their hopes and their lives in his hands. He could not rest now, when only twenty-nine miles separated him from rescue for his men.

He would take Worsley and Crean, and leave McCarthy to look after McNeish and Vincent. They would travel light. They would take no sleeping bags, planning to go fast, with quick rests. They would carry sledging rations and biscuits for three days of travel. They would take the Primus camp stove and three days of fuel. They had an ax. They had fifty feet of rope from scraps knotted together. They had Worsley's compass and an outline map of South Georgia that showed the coastline in detail and a complete blank in the interior of the island.

On May 18, with a full moon shining at 2:00 A.M., the Boss decided it was time to go. He roused Worsley. "We'll get under way now, Skipper."

THE ALPS OF THE SOUTHERN OCEAN

Shackleton, Worsley, and Crean set off, climbing toward a pass through ankle-deep snow. Still tired and out of condition from their long months of confinement and their voyages, the men found the hiking a strain. Worsley continued to navigate. Laying their outline map of the island on the snow with the compass, he would sight ahead to a distant pass or peak and take a bearing by that. Four miles from their starting point, they had to rope up for security. The footing was sometimes tricky, and all were weak. Deep crevasses snaked across their path from time to time. Shackleton went in the lead, breaking the trail.

"The bright moonlight showed us that the interior was tremendously broken," Shackleton wrote. "High peaks, impassable cliffs, steep snow-slopes, and sharply descending glaciers could be seen in all directions, with stretches of snow-plain overlaying the ice sheet of the interior."

To avoid tiring themselves, the Boss decided they should make a brief halt every fifteen minutes. They threw themselves on their backs and caught their breath, looking up at the mist-covered mountains gleaming white in the moonlight, and sucked on handfuls of snow to ease their thirst. After two minutes, they would haul themselves up again and continue. At eight o'clock, the sun rose, and as they continued tramping steadily upward toward the great range of mountains in their path, the only sound was the crunch of their footsteps in the snow.

They were making for a pass they had spotted. By noon they reached its summit. Breathing hard, sweating with the effort of hiking through knee-deep snow, they pulled themselves up and peered over. On the other side was a sheer drop. Icefalls glittered in the sun below them as a hard breeze buffeted their faces. There was nothing to do but go back down the way they had come, and angle off toward the next pass.

Halfway up to the next gap, Shackleton called a halt for a meal. They ate on the snow, their chests heaving. Then they pushed themselves up again, and struggled on to the next gap. The way down the other side was just as impossible, and their hearts sank with disappointment. Swallowing their dismay, they

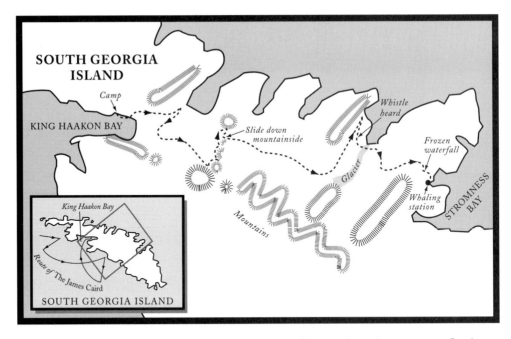

SOUTH GEORGIA
ISLAND

KING HAAKON BAY

Camp

Slide down
mountainside

Whistle
heard

Frozen
waterfall

Glacier

Whaling
station

STROMNESS
BAY

Mountains

King Haakon Bay

Route of The James Caird

SOUTH GEORGIA ISLAND

Based on a sketch by Shackleton, this map shows the route across South
Georgia taken by Shackleton, Worsley, and Crean.

trudged down through their own footsteps and began flanking the next peak to
reach another pass. They were about 4,000 feet above sea level, and the temperature was as Alpine as the terrain.

As they slogged their way through the snow, a strange feeling began to grow
on each of the men. The three discovered long afterward that they all had the
feeling that there was a fourth. "Even now I again find myself counting our
party—Shackleton, Crean, and I and—who was the other?" Worsley wrote
later. "Of course, there were only three, but it is strange that in mentally review-
ing the crossing we should always think of a fourth, and then correct ourselves."

"When I look back at those days," Shackleton added, "I do not doubt that
Providence guided us . . . I know that during that long march of thirty-six hours
over the unnamed mountains and glaciers of South Georgia it often seemed to
me that we were four, not three." Later, some people found religious significance
in the men's experience. Others put "the Fourth Presence" down to the psycho-
logical and physical strain the men were under.

At the time, however, Shackleton, Worsley, and Crean did not discuss it. Together the three men dragged themselves up to the third pass. For the third time, they found that they could not make the descent on the other side. They gritted their teeth and trudged down again. A long snowfield lay between them and the next gap, and on crossing it they discovered a crevasse so deep that "two battleships could have been hidden in it," as Worsley said. They zigzagged to the right and reached the saddle of the fourth pass as night fell.

"We'll try it," Shackleton said.

He started down, cutting steps in the ice with the ax. Sea fog was sweeping in behind them, and the light was fading quickly. They crept down 200 yards, feeling the angle of the slope grow easier with each step. Shackleton paused to let Worsley and Crean catch up with him, coiling the slack rope between them as they came.

Below them the snowy slope disappeared in the darkness. They had no idea where it ended, if it dropped off into space or came to rest in a snowfield. At the speed they were climbing down, they could not get off the peak that night. To be trapped at the summit, where the wind was coldest and strongest, was too dangerous. They would surely freeze to death.

The men peered ahead. Shackleton gave them each an inquiring look, and then said again, "We'll try it. It's a devil of a risk, but we've got to take it."

Worsley and Crean were shocked. The Boss, normally so cautious, was suggesting they *slide* down the mountain.

"What if we hit a rock?" Crean asked.

"Can we stay where we are?" Shackleton replied.

"What if the slope doesn't level off?" Worsley wondered aloud.

Shackleton's voice rose a bit. "Can we stay where we are?"

The men had no answer for him.

Silently, they placed their coiled ropes underneath them and sat in a line with their knees around the man in front—tobogganers with no toboggan. "And so, locked together, we let go," Worsley wrote. "I was never more scared in my life than for the first thirty seconds. The speed was terrific. I think we all gasped at the hair-raising shoot into darkness . . . Then, to our joy, the slope curved out, and we shot into a bank of soft snow. We estimated we had shot down a mile in two or three minutes, and had lowered our altitude by two or three thousand feet. We stood up and shook hands—very pleased with ourselves."

They moved on a bit from the bottom of the slope, just in case they had triggered an avalanche. Then they got the Primus going and boiled down some snow so they could cook their hoosh. They had one cook pot and three spoons, and when the hoosh was ready they took turns dipping their spoons in one at a time.

"Crean's got the largest spoon," Shackleton complained jokingly.

"Holy smoke, look at the skipper's mouth!" Crean shot back.

Worsley took advantage of the argument to get an extra dig into the pot with his spoon.

From months of training they were able to eat their hoosh boiling hot. The warmth spread through their shivering bodies, giving them the energy to start marching again. They had been hiking for sixteen hours.

They were making their way steadily eastward through the razorbacks that formed South Georgia's spine. The moon began to rise behind the mountains ahead of them, showing them the way through another pass. By midnight they were at the top and looking down at a long ocean bay. By two in the morning, they were down far enough to see rocky islets below them. They couldn't be sure what bay they were looking at, however, and to be sure of hitting the whaling stations, they kept to the east.

As they descended, they found themselves in an area riddled with crevasses and realized they were on a glacier. Judging it too risky to cross in the dark, Shackleton turned to march them around it. At five, they called a halt halfway up another slope. Worsley and Crean began to nod off.

"I'll wake you in half an hour," Shackleton said.

He kept watch, not daring to go to sleep. All his experience in the Antarctic had proven to him that going to sleep under those conditions could be his last act. When ten minutes had passed, he nudged his companions awake.

"You've been asleep for thirty minutes," he said.

Worsley and Crean shook themselves, as refreshed as if they actually *had* slept for half an hour. Shackleton's lie gave them twenty minutes of fantasy sleep. The men stood and braced themselves to push forward, up the steep grade. Some time after six o'clock they reached the gap.

Although it was still dark, they could make out the white shape of the land stretched out below them. To the east they recognized Stromness Bay. Their destination was actually in sight. Crean fussed with the Primus stove as Shackleton and Worsley surveyed the terrain. Then Crean called out "Hoosh!" and the men gathered around the pot with their spoons.

"What's the time?" Shackleton asked Worsley.

The skipper pulled his chronometer out from beneath his shirt. "Six fifty-five."

"We'll listen for the whaling station's whistle," Shackleton said.

They waited, almost holding their breath in the still, frigid air. The minutes ticked by. They watched the hands on the chronometer creep toward seven o'clock, and then from far below came a distant blast of the factory whistle.

The three men shook hands and laughed. No music had ever sounded so sweet to their ears.

"It was a moment hard to describe," Shackleton wrote later. "Pain and aches, boat journeys, marches, hunger and fatigue seemed to belong to the limbo of forgotten things, and there remained only the perfect contentment that comes of work accomplished."

The fuel for the camp stove was finished, and so they threw it aside. But there were still miles to go before the safety of the whaling station. They did not celebrate for long.

Below them a steep, icy slope slanted downward. Day after day, the winter sun had melted the snow on the eastward-facing slope, and the night frosts had hardened it, until it was a solid, frozen, glittering wall. Shackleton chopped steps in the ice and they inched their way down. When the slope eased a little bit, they lowered themselves down on their backs, kicking in heel holds as they descended for a thousand feet to the sea. Gentoo penguins and elephant seals ogled them as they began clambering over boulders along the shore.

They kept to the coast for several miles, sometimes struggling over ice and snow, sometimes trudging through deep sand and around rocks. For a while the only sounds were the scrabbling of their boots over the rocks, their own harsh breathing, and the occasional belch or bellow from an elephant seal. Then when a glacier blocked their path, they had to turn inland again, wearily climbing uphill. At one fifteen they were staring down onto Stromness Bay from a 3,000-foot summit. Below them two whaling ships were as tiny as insects. Worsley yelled and waved in a futile attempt to draw attention to them. Shackleton led the way downward.

Soon they found themselves following a stream of snowmelt through a narrow ravine. The sides of the gully drew closer and closer together until the three men were forced to slosh through the glacial water, sometimes up to their knees. Then the ravine came to an abrupt end. The water poured away into space. Cautiously, the men stepped to the edge and looked down.

Below them was a frozen waterfall stretching fifty feet to the ground. Unless they wanted to splash back upstream for a mile and find another route, they would have to climb down the waterfall.

There was nothing to tie the rope to. Worsley held it, while first Shackleton and then Crean went over the edge. They went down the rope as sailors do, letting it slip through their hands and not putting their weight on it until just before they hit bottom. At the top, Worsley bunched the end of the rope up and jammed it under some rocks. If he didn't put his weight on the rope until the bottom, it might just hold.

Worsley stepped off into the air, plummeting downward with the rope whipping through his hands. Shackleton and Crean caught him as he fell, and his full weight yanked on the rope. It held.

Startled, the three men stared up at the top of the waterfall and tugged on the rope. It wouldn't budge. It might have been frozen, but they couldn't understand what was holding it. Shrugging, they turned and left their rope hanging where it was. They didn't need it any longer.

They had a few miles of frozen marsh to cross, and then they were within sight of the whaling station. So far no one had spotted them.

"Boss, there might be some women here," Worsley said nervously.

"What of it?"

"Well, look at us," Worsley replied.

They were three scarecrows, their clothes in tatters, their faces black with soot and grease, their hair and beards matted. They hadn't bathed in months, and they had been living in the same clothes since abandoning ship. They came around the corner of a building and startled two Norwegian boys, who took one look at them and bolted. Around the men was the familiar pervasive stench of the whaling factory—smelling almost as bad as they did themselves.

Staggering slightly, shaking with deep chills, Shackleton, Worsley, and Crean climbed the steps of the factory manager's house. A foreman came to the door.

"Captain Sørlle? Is he here?" Shackleton asked hoarsely.

"What do you want?" the man replied in English, eyeing them with amazement.

"I want to see him. I know him," Shackleton answered.

The foreman went inside, and a few moments later Captain Sørlle came out to look at them. They had last seen him a year and a half earlier, when he had toasted *Endurance* and her crew.

"Do you know me, Sørlle?" Shackleton asked the big Norwegian whaler.

"No. Who the hell are you?" Sørlle demanded.

"My name is Shackleton."

Sørlle gaped in astonishment at the three ragged castaways, and then turned his head away and wept. What Shackleton did not know was that *Aurora*, the relief ship that had been sent to meet him, had met a similar fate to *Endurance*. It, too, had been trapped in the ice since the previous year, and although not crushed it was badly damaged. Just weeks earlier, on March 24, 1916, an ominous message from her radio had been picked up in Australia: HULL SEVERELY STRAINED. SHIP RELEASED FROM ICE MARCH 14TH . . . WIRELESS APPEALS FOR RELIEF SHIP SENT DURING WINTER NO ACKNOWLEDGMENT. SHIP PROCEEDING PORT CHALMERS, NEW ZEALAND. JURY RUDDER NO ANCHORS SHORT OF FUEL. *Aurora* was limping away, and the headlines in the London papers read: IS SHACKLETON SAFE? MYSTERY OF THE GREAT WHITE SOUTH. Everyone had assumed that Shackleton's team was trekking overland, only to find themselves abandoned.

Now, Shackleton, Worsley, and Crean stood dazed and exhausted—not on the edge of Antarctica, but on South Georgia Island—the last place anyone expected to find them. They could hardly believe what they had just done, and they were as overcome with emotion as Sørlle was.

"It was like this," Shackleton said much later. "The thought of those fellows on Elephant Island kept us going all the time. It might have been different if we'd had only ourselves to think about. You can get so tired in the snow, particularly if you're hungry, that sleep seems just the best thing life has to give . . . But if you're a leader, a fellow that other fellows look to, you've got to keep going. That was the thought which sailed us through the hurricane and tugged us up and down those mountains . . . and when we got to the whaling station, it was the thought of those comrades which made us so mad with joy that the reaction beats all effort to describe it. We didn't so much feel that we were safe as that they were saved."

Sørlle put his arms around the three weary men and ushered them tenderly into the house.

Shackleton, Worsley, and Crean were given hot baths and food and then taken to a bedroom, where they collapsed. They slept the night through, sometimes shouting out in nightmare terrors of great waves or danger on the ice. The Norwegians at the whaling factory crowded Sørlle's house, asking the manager over and over again to repeat the story Shackleton had told. Even for men accustomed to a hard life in a terrifying ocean, they could hardly believe what Shackleton and his men had endured.

The next morning, Worsley was taken aboard a whale-catcher called *Samson* and went to King Haakon Bay to rescue McCarthy, McNeish, and Vincent. "We thought the skipper would have come back," McCarthy grumbled as a clean-shaven Worsley jumped out onto the beach.

"Well, I am here," Worsley said with a laugh, and the other men stared in disbelief.

The *James Caird* was brought on board as well, and the whalemen treated the boat like a priceless object. They were men who knew the heroism of the boat itself.

Back at the whaling station, Shackleton was busy organizing a ship to set out for Elephant Island. Telegrams were already racing across the oceans. SIR ERNEST SHACKLETON SAFE! ran the headlines. The story of the

Endurance crew's remarkable ordeal was already dinner conversation in London.

But the Boss had no idea what he would find when he returned to the desolate spot where he had left his men.

CAMP WILD

As the twenty-two men left on Elephant Island watched the *James Caird* disappear among the ice on April 24, most of them felt an overwhelming gloom begin to settle. They had no illusions about Shackleton's chances. But they could not stand brooding in the chilly rain. Wild, in charge, would not let them fall into helplessness and despair; that would have been the same as admitting they were doomed.

Their new commander decided that their first priority was shelter. Their tents had been lashed to ribbons by the violent wind, and they were all suffering from exposure. Some of the men were useless for work: Rickinson had suffered a heart attack, and Blackborrow could not walk. Some of the others were in a stupor of exhaustion and could hardly stand. So, weakened by their ordeal and suffering from frostbite, the rest of the crew began constructing a hut with the only materials available. They collected rocks and built walls four feet high, and then turned the *Docker* and the *Wills* over to form a roof. Over the top went one of the last remaining sails, lashed down and secured with more rocks. If they had been rested and strong, they could have built their shelter in an hour. As it was, it took them nearly a day.

When it was done, the men took their sodden sleeping bags and crawled into their new hut. The seats of the upside-down boats formed a second story inside, and some of the crew installed themselves up there. Inside it was dark and only slightly warmer than outside. Wind constantly found its way through the chinks in the rocks walls forcing in snow. At first, when they tried to cook inside with one of the blubber stoves, the oily smoke nearly suffocated the men. But Kerr took the metal lining from one of the cases of biscuits and fashioned a chimney of sorts. It didn't draw all of the smoke, but it was some improvement. Occasionally, a gust of wind swooped down through the vent and forced a cloud of choking blubber smoke into the cramped space, driving the men outside to gasp for air. Soon everyone and everything inside was covered with a layer of greasy soot, but the stove provided much-needed warmth, and the men were beyond caring how dirty they were. A few

The hut—built from the overturned hulls of the *Wills* and the *Docker*—in which Wild and the remaining crew survived the winter of 1916.

of them made seal-oil lamps, which gave a weak light that was just barely enough for reading.

Outside, the weather grew worse. Gale winds blew snow from the peaks of Elephant Island and drifted it high against the sides of the hut. On calm days the island was enveloped in cold, wet mist, and the offshore ice crowded against the rocky beach. May brought blizzards so severe that Wild was afraid their hut would be smashed by the sheets of ice that the wind wrenched from the cliffs.

When the weather permitted, the crew kept busy catching penguins, which were numerous and noisy in the nearby rookery. From time to time, a seal lumbered onto the rocky shore and was quickly killed. The glacier that hung from the cliffs at their backs was their reservoir of water: chipping ice and bringing it inside to melt on the stove was a critical job.

But otherwise, there was nothing they could actually do to improve their circumstances. They just had to wait for Shackleton's return. At first the men had speculated about how soon they could possibly expect a rescue ship. Nobody ever stepped outside the hut without casting a quick look seaward. But as the weeks dragged on and the winter locked up the ocean around Elephant Island, they knew they were stuck until spring.

Inside the hut, life went on. Wild was lenient with the men, knowing that being too strict would make their hard life even more unbearable. Dr. Macklin and Dr. McIlroy were kept busy with teeth that needed pulling, infections that needed treatment, saltwater sores that needed attention. The most important medical task that faced them was Blackborrow's frostbitten toes. His right foot recovered, but on his left foot gangrene had set in in the toes. McIlroy kept an eye on the condition, waiting until it was clear that the gangrene would not spread, and that a scar of new tissue had grown between the rotten toes and the rest of Blackborrow's foot. Then it was time to operate.

The hoosh pot was cleaned and scoured, filled with ice to melt, and once the water was boiling, the surgical instruments were sterilized. All the seal-oil lamps were lit, making the hut as bright as possible, and the patient was laid on an operating table of packing crates. Macklin uncorked a bottle of chloroform and dampened some gauze with it. "Breathe deep," he told Blackborrow as he held it over the young man's nose.

McIlroy took the scalpel from the boiling water and began cutting away the toes. One by one, they dropped into a tin can with a dull *plink,* and the surgeon then began sewing up the wound. The whole operation took just under an hour.

Aside from medical procedures, life in the hut was uneventful. The men took turns reading the few books they had left. They rolled cigarettes of dried grass in pages of the encyclopedia. They mended their clothes by lamplight. They marked the days as they dragged by. On June 22, they celebrated Midwinter's Day again, although not as comfortably as the last year's party on board *Endurance.* They threw a little bit of everything from the dwindling food stores into the hoosh pot for dinner and had a round of singing to Hussey's banjo. Kerr gave an encore performance of "Spagoni the Toreador" for oldtimes' sake, but the greatest applause of the evening went to James, who composed a song he performed for the occasion:

> *"My name is Frankie Wild-o, my hut's on Elephant Isle.*
> *The wall's without a single brick, the roof's without a tile.*
> *But nevertheless, you must confess, for many and many a mile,*
> *It's the most palatial dwelling place you'll find on Elephant Isle."*

One ritual the men looked forward to was hearing a recipe from a small paperback cookbook that Marston had. Each night he read one recipe aloud to the crew, and at the end of the recitation the men spent hours discussing the recipe, comparing it to others they had known, reminiscing about meals they had enjoyed back home.

Food had become an obsession with them. Each man had a daily sugar ration of three lumps, but most of them willingly put one lump a day in the "sugar pool." At the end of seven days, the man whose turn it was got all the sugar at once. Food was traded to get out of chores: no one liked going outside into the cold to get frozen meat for the hoosh pot, but bartering a penguin steak could usually get a man out of the job. There was always someone willing to take the extra chore for the extra food. Clark was so fed up with the daily

Saved!

diet of penguin hoosh that he began searching the shore for *anything* else that could be eaten; occasionally he found limpets (a kind of mollusk) and an edible variety of seaweed to add to the pot. Some of the men worried that the penguins would all disappear one day, migrating off the island that the men had begun to call Hell-ephan Island.

The penguins did not disappear. They seemed to be stuck on Elephant Island along with the men. As the weeks lengthened into months of captivity, the men could not help feeling twinges of despair. But every morning the ever-optimistic Wild rolled up his sleeping bag and said to the men, "Get your things ready, boys. The Boss may come today."

"Today" finally came on August 30, more than four months after the *James Caird* had sailed away. Marston, walking along the beach, spotted the smoke from a ship's funnel. "Ship ho!" he cried hoarsely, running to the hut.

One by one the men emerged from the shelter, straining to see. Hurriedly, they ignited a signal fire with dried grass and seal blubber. They dragged their remaining stores and gear to the beach, waving their arms and shouting to the ship.

It was a Chilean steamer, the *Yelcho*. The vessel stopped, and a boat was lowered over the side.

"I felt jolly near blubbing for a bit," Wild said later, "and could not speak for several minutes." He had recognized the Boss. Worsley and Crean were at his side.

As soon as the boat got within shouting distance, Shackleton called out, "Are all well?"

"Yes!" someone shouted back. "Are *you* all well?"

"Don't we look all right now that we've washed?" the Boss replied.

The men on the beach were laughing and hugging one another. As soon as the boat was grounded, Shackleton ordered a hasty departure.

"We knew you'd come back," one of the men said to him.

As the Boss said later, it was the highest compliment he had ever been paid. He had been trying desperately for four months to get a rescue ship to Elephant Island. Each time, the winter ice had turned him back. Each time, he had been forced to return to South America, not knowing if his men were alive or dead. But he had finally arrived to take them home.

And they had all survived.

On each of his three expeditions to explore the Antarctic, Shackleton had failed in his mission. And yet what he and his crew *did* succeed in doing in 1915–1916 was one of the most incredible feats of survival ever recorded. Every stage of their journey seemed more remarkable than the last. From January 1915, when *Endurance* was trapped in the ice, during its helpless drift through the Weddell Sea and its destruction in October, to the crew's long, miserable months of camping on the ice, the Boss had held his men together under terrible conditions. Their three-boat passage in April 1916 to Elephant

Members of the *Endurance* expedition photographed in Punta Arenas, Chile, after their rescue. The uniformed figure is the captain of the rescue ship. From left to right: Hussey, Hurley, Kerr, James, Wordie, Crean, Worsley, Wild, Shackleton, Captain Pardo, Orde-Lees, Marston, How, Holness, Stevenson, Bakewell, Green, McLeod, Cheetham.

Island was accomplished in spite of enormous odds. The voyage of the *James Caird* over 800 miles of winter ocean rivals any small-boat journey in history. Shackleton's trek across the unmapped peaks of South Georgia was the first in that hostile mountain range, and the survival of the crew in their hut on Elephant Island over one Antarctic winter is almost too much to believe.

And yet it all happened. Shackleton brought them all home.

EPILOGUE

World War I was still raging when the ice men returned to England. Almost to a man, they joined their countrymen at war. Sadly, after surviving their ordeal in the Antarctic, several of them were killed in action, among them McCarthy and Cheetham, two of the most cheerful and well-liked members of the whole group.

With his cold-weather experience, Shackleton was given command of a unit in North Russia. He took Worsley, Hussey, and Macklin with him.

At the end of the war, life returned to normal, and Shackleton began a world tour, speaking to audiences in big cities and outback villages about *Endurance*'s doomed voyage. He had accomplished one of the most spectacular feats of survival ever recorded, and he was celebrated on every continent.

And yet, as always, it was the southern continent that called him. He had never been comfortable in civilization. He yearned for the frozen south again. In 1921, he gathered a crew together to return to the Antarctic on the *Quest*. The goal for this voyage was to circumnavigate the continent and map all the islands that were still uncharted. At his side were Frank Wild, Alexander Macklin, Frank Worsley, James McIlroy, Leonard Hussey, Charles Green, Thomas McLeod, and A.J. Kerr.

They sailed for the south. But Shackleton's many years of exploration had finally broken his health. As the *Quest* leaped forward over the waves, he began to look very sick. Macklin and McIlroy, the doctors, tried to get him to slow down, but he was obstinate. At port in Rio de Janeiro, the Boss suffered a heart attack and took to his bed. But he would not go home. The ship kept on south until it reached South Georgia Island.

On January 5, 1922, the *Quest* sailed into Grytviken Harbor and dropped anchor. As always, the air was filled with the smell of rotting whale carcasses and the sound of elephant seals bellowing and belching on the beach. Late in the night, with the summer twilight still brightening the sky, Dr. Macklin was called to Shackleton's cabin. Shackleton had had another heart attack.

"You'll have to change your way of life, Boss," Macklin said.

"You're always wanting me to give up things. What is it I ought to give up?"

The one thing he had truly to give up was the Antarctic, and that he could not do. He died a few minutes after Macklin came to him.

He was buried there, on South Georgia Island.

Here's to the long white road that beckons,

The climb that baffles, the risk that nerves.

And here's to the merry heart that reckons

The rough with the smooth and never swerves.

—from a New Zealand school song,
one of Shackleton's favorites

ACKNOWLEDGMENTS

I used many books and sources in writing this text. The most important books on Shackleton and the Imperial Trans-Antarctic Expedition were: *Endurance,* by Alfred Lansing; *Shackleton's Boat Journey,* by Frank Worsley; *Shackleton,* by Roland Huntford; and Shackleton's own writings in *South.* For general information on the Antarctic, I used *Antarctica, the Last Continent,* by Ian Cameron; *A Natural History of the Antarctic: Life in the Freezer,* by Alastair Fotherhill; and *Below the Convergence: Voyages Toward Antarctica 1699–1839,* by Alan Gurney, among other useful books.

The most significant and rewarding assistance I received was at the Scott Polar Research Institute, in Cambridge, England, from Dr. Robert Headland, Shirley Sawtell, and Philippa Hogg. They gave me complete access to the institute's impressive library and the archival material relating to *Endurance.* After researching the expedition for so long, the experience of examining Worsley's precious logbook and Frank Hurley's original photographs in Cambridge was a true thrill. All the photographs in this book are reproductions of Hurley's pictures, used by permission of SPRI.

BIBLIOGRAPHY

ANTARCTICA, NAVIGATION, AND GENERAL

Blewitt, Mary. *Celestial Navigation for Yachtsmen.* Camden, Maine: International Marine, 1964.

Bowman, Gerald. *Men of the Antarctic.* New York: Fleet Publishing, 1959.

Boy Scouts of America, *The Sea Explorer Manual.* New Brunswick, New Jersey: BSA National Council, 1958.

Cameron, Ian. *Antarctica: The Last Continent.* Boston: Little, Brown and Co., 1974.

Campbell, David G. *The Crystal Desert: Summers in Antarctica.* New York: Houghton Mifflin, 1992.

Dennis, Jerry. *The Bird in the Waterfall: A Natural History of Oceans, Rivers, and Lakes.* New York: HarperCollins, 1996.

Fotherhill, Alastair. *A Natural History of the Antarctic: Life in the Freezer.* New York: Sterling Publishing Co., 1993.

Gurney, Alan. *Below the Convergence: Voyages Toward Antarctica 1699–1839.* New York: W.W. Norton and Company, 1997.

May, John. *The Greenpeace Book of Antarctica: A New View of the Seventh Continent.* New York: Doubleday & Co., 1988.

Naveen, Ron, Colin Monteath, Tui De Roy, and Mark Jones. *Wild Ice: Antarctic Journeys.* Washington, D.C.: Smithsonian Institution Press, 1990.

Sobel, Dava. *Longitude: The True Story of a Lone Genius Who Solved the Greatest Scientific Problem of His Time.* New York: Walker Publishing, 1995.

Steger, Will and Jon Bowermaster. *Crossing Antarctica.* New York: Alfred A. Knopf, 1992.

SHACKLETON

Begbie, Harold. *Shackleton: A Memory.* London: Mills and Boon Ltd., 1922.

Chidsey, Donald. *Shackleton's Voyage.* London: Tandem Books, 1967.

Fisher, Margery and Fisher, James. *Shackleton and the Antarctic.* Boston: Houghton Mifflin Company, 1957.

Huntford, Roland. *Shackleton.* New York: Atheneum, 1986.

Hurley, Frank. *Shackleton's Argonauts.* Sydney: Angus and Robertson, 1948.

Hussey, Leonard. *South with Shackleton.* London: Sampson Low, 1949.

Lansing, Alfred. *Endurance: Shackleton's Incredible Voyage.* New York: McGraw-Hill Book Co., Ltd., 1959.

McNeish, Harry. *Endurance* diaries. Collection of SPRI, Cambridge, England.

Mill, Hugh Robert. *The Life of Sir Ernest Shackleton.* London: William Heinemann Ltd., 1923.

Shackleton, Sir Ernest Henry. *Shackleton: His Antarctic Writings Selected and Introduced by Christopher Ralling.* London: British Broadcasting Corporation, 1983.

Shackleton, Sir Ernest Henry. *South.* London: William Heinemann Ltd., 1919.

Worsley, F.A. *Endurance: An Epic of Polar Adventure.* London: Philip Allan, 1931.

Worsley, F.A. *Shackleton's Boat Journey.* New York: W.W. Norton and Company, Inc., 1977.

Worsley, Frank. *Endurance* diaries. Collection of SPRI, Cambridge, England.

PERIODICALS

Antarctic News Bulletin, No. 11 (September 1953); No. 13 (March 1954); No. 18 (June 1955).

British Medical Journal, Vol. 307 (December 1993).

Geographical Journal, Vol. 138 No.3 (1972). "Joint Services Expedition to Elephant Island."

Jones, A.G.E. "Frankie Wild's Hut." *Falkland Islands Journal* (1982).

Polar Record, Vol. 29, No. 169 (April 1993); Vol. No. 71 (1962); Vol. 33, No. 184, (January 1997).

Wordie, J.M. "The Drift of the *Endurance.*" *Geographical Journal,* Vol. LI, No. 4 (April 1918).

INDEX

JENNIFER ARMSTRONG is the author of many books for young readers, including *The Dreams of Mairhe Mehan, Mary Mehan Awake, Pockets, Chin Yu Min and the Ginger Cat,* and *Black-Eyed Susan.* She lives in Saratoga Springs, New York.